To Pine Crest
School

Best Wishe

Rae Halpen

The Light Behind the Window

by
Rae Halpern

Shengold Publishers, Inc.
New York

ISBN 0-88400-155-5
Library of Congress Catalog Card Number: 91-053047
Copyright © 1991 by Rae Halpern

Shengold Publishers, Inc.
18 West 45th Street, New York, NY 10036

Printed in the United States of America

To my Mother, whose love nurtured me;
my Husband, Harry, whose love strengthened me;
my Children, Eva, Jack and Lexi;
and my Grandchildren, Jordan and Lauren, whose love and
sweetness helped heal my wounds.

Contents

Introduction

Dear Lauren and Jordan,

I want to thank you for the best birthday party of my life. It must have been the first time that "My Little Pony" decorated the party of a sixty-one-year-old grandma. As for me, it was my first officially celebrated theme birthday party.

I loved the menu, the decorations, the table setting, the presents, and the entertainment. But, most of all, Lauren, you made me very happy when you promised, in the role of Fairy Godmother, that I would be present at your wedding. Being enveloped in all the love that flowed from you and Jordan and your Mom and Dad, I was touched by your childhood innocence and truly believed that you had the power to grant me this wonderful gift.

However, I am a realistic being, who knows this may not be possible; life is so unpredictable. There are so many things I would like to tell you, Lauren and Jordan. You may not fully understand them all just now, but since I may not have the chance later, when you are older, I've decided to put it all on paper so that, one day in the future, you can read and appreciate the story of my life.

I would not like you to remember me only as the Grandma who went on vacations and brought back T-shirts and presents, or who ate in fancy restaurants, gave parties and generally lived a good life full of prosperity and affluence in her old age. Nor do I want you to remember me simply as a Grandma whose breath may not have smelled as sweet as T.V. commercials dictated. Though I am all those things, and thank God for allowing me to enjoy the good life, it was not always so. I would like to tell you about the other side of my life as well.

Darling Jordan, you often asked me who my mother and father were and what had become of my brothers and sisters. I always avoided the answer, because I felt that you, who were brought up in a normal, happy, secure home with two parents and two siblings might not understand the type of family I grew up in. But I will try now to paint, for you, my grandchildren, a picture of my childhood.

Chapter 1

A Child in Uzhorod, Czechoslovakia

My mother's father was a prosperous merchant and leading citizen in our community. He had sixteen children; my mother was the youngest. All her brothers and sisters were married and each had many children. My grandparents had so many grandchildren that they could not keep track of them. Because my mother was the youngest, and I came along late in her life, I was their youngest grandchild. Most of my cousins were much older than I was. As a matter of fact, my grandparents had many great-grandchildren who were older than I was!

Here are two pictures that were taken at a wedding of one of my cousins. One shows my grandparents with most of my uncles and aunts. The other picture is of many of my cousins. You can see that my grandparents are very old in this picture, and it was taken two years before I was born!

My father was a Hebrew scholar. When his father's grain business went bankrupt during the First World War, he fell back on the only things he knew—the Talmud and Torah—and became a Hebrew teacher. He was a very pious, intelligent man and very knowledgeable about world affairs as well. This was a rare combination for pious Jews in those days.

My father's life was devoted to the Torah. By day he taught it, and the rest of the time, he studied it. His head was always in one book or another. As soon as we had finished dinner and cleared the table, he took out one of the books that lined our walls. He sat there and studied late into the night. He was gentle and mild-mannered, absorbed in the synagogue and his studies. He was highly respected in our community.

We were long on respect and short on cash. My mother's first husband had died of typhoid fever, which was rampant in Europe during and right after the First World War, and she was left with four small children. My father's first wife died about the same time. Since he was much older than my mother, four of

At a cousin's wedding in 1923. My grandparents are seated in the center. My mother is standing behind my grandmother. The others are Mother's siblings and their spouses, five of whom died of natural causes. The rest perished in Auschwitz.

At the same wedding, my grandmother, seated next to the bride, is surrounded by her grandchildren. All but five of these perished in the Holocaust.

his five children were already married and living on their own. He and my mother married and, a few years later, I was born.

Whenever anybody asked me how many brothers and sisters I had, I didn't know what to answer. I thought, "Shall I say I am an only child?" In a sense, I really was an only child, because I was the only child my parents had together. "Or shall I count the siblings on my father's side, whom I hardly know, or the ones on my mother's side?" All this was confused by the fact that the children on each side were bitter enemies, forever feuding and fighting, and I was always in the middle. Since I grew up with my mother's children, I decided to count only them. There was my sister, Piri, who was fourteen when I was born; Lenke, twelve; my brother, Moishe, ten; and Gershon, seven. Add to that my father's daughter, who lived with us, and you can see what a busy household we had. The apartment we lived in consisted of two rooms and a kitchen. One large room served as the living room–bedroom–dining room. Our walls were lined with homemade bookshelves full of old books of all shapes and sizes. They contained the Talmud, Mishnas, and Tanach, all in Hebrew.

I told you before that the "My Little Pony" birthday party you gave me was my first. I would like to tell you about other "firsts" that came to me late in life.

The first real birthday present I ever received was from Grandpa after we were married—the gold locket I now give to you, Lauren. The first new coat I ever got was when I was sixteen—the same year that I bought my first toothbrush. Until I married Grandpa, I never had my own room; I didn't even have my own bed.

I know what you are thinking: "Ridiculous! That nutty Grandma is making up stories again! How can you be without your own bed?" You would be surprised how many things you take for granted that I and other children did without—and still do.

Then where did I sleep? Since I was the smallest, I slept either with my mother, my brother or sister—wherever there was room. We slept "Zu fusens" (literally translated, "by the feet"). In other words, we put pillows on each end of the bed and my head would be next to someone else's feet. Often I would fall asleep in one bed, and wake up in another. I did not have to worry about where I left my pajamas; I did not have any. We had few personal possessions and very little privacy.

*I am sitting on my mother's lap. Behind us, from left to right, are my sisters
Lenke, Kornelia and Piri. Behind Father are my brothers Moishe and
Gershon. Photo taken in 1927.*

From the time I was born until I was about ten years old, we
lived in that apartment. It sat in a long courtyard, occupied by
about fifteen families. Most of them were poor or temporarily
impoverished like us. At the end of that courtyard, there was a
house of worship (a small synagogue).

None of us had indoor plumbing, central heating, gas stoves
or even electricity in the beginning. (Some of the well-to-do
people in town did.) We had to bring clean water in from the
well outside and dump the dirty water outside in the sewers.
Also, we had to bring the wood for cooking our food and heating our apartment in from the shed. Both of these chores fell
early on me and I remember slipping and falling often around
the frozen well, with pails of water in hand.

No plumbing also meant outdoor toilets. In our case, we had
eight wooden latrines for the whole courtyard. I must also tell
you that they were unheated and I remember freezing my you-
know-what. The Gypsies would empty the latrines from time to
time. Until then, everything just sat there and smelled to high
heaven.

Since our courtyard was unenclosed and led into two public

streets, our unlocked latrines were used by many strangers who passed by. Because the aim of these strangers as they relieved themselves was often not very good, the first rule we had for using the latrine was, "Before you sit down, make sure you are not about to sit on something the previous occupant has left!" It was a far cry from our color-coordinated, tiled bathrooms, with matching towels and toilet paper on each floor! And as for toilet paper—there wasn't any. I remember scrounging for newspaper (which was scarce) and settling for a piece of a brown paper bag, which I would rub between my fingers to make it less hard and scratchy.

So you see, we had very few creature comforts, but we did not mind because everyone in the courtyard had the same two rooms, and some had even larger families than ours. In addition, some of the tradesmen worked at home, so in the daytime the courtyard housed to a bustling cottage industry.

We had few factories that could mass produce the things we needed. Because it was very costly to bring in everything from the more industrialized western part of Czechoslovakia, we made things ourselves. Tinsmiths made potbellied stoves; carpenters made furniture; dressmakers, tailors, and lingerie makers sewed clothes; candy makers produced candies and chocolates. Most of this merchandise was offered for sale from stalls at the market. Sometimes things were made to order. If a certain tradesman prospered, he would open a shop or store, but every one of these businesses originated in the home, as with the "cottages" of the British Isles. This way the family could help out and there would be no overhead.

Our next-door neighbors were the Grunbergers. Mr. Grunberger was a bookbinder. During the day, their bedroom became a workshop. He and his son worked all day by the window, making use of the sunlight. They bound new books and repaired old ones that the people from the town and vicinity brought to them. Their place always smelled of glue and old books. We would come in and watch them work. They would let us help them hold the books and, as a reward, they would give us scrap paper and paste.

Another neighbor, a widower, lived with his spinster daughter, who kept an immaculate house and took care of her father. He was a scribe, and every day from morning to night he would sit by the window with a long quill and inscribe mezzuzas or a Torah. He had the most beautiful Hebrew handwriting; his letters were perfect, like matched pearls. Children would stand in front of his window and watch him, but he never looked up. He was a very pious Jew and was transfixed when he worked. He and his daughter were as poor as church mice.

Across from them, in one big room, lived the Reitters. Mr. and Mrs. Reitter and their two daughters lived in the back of the room. In front was a big machine on which Mr. Reitter, a carpenter, worked knee deep in sawdust and wood shavings. He carved wooden legs for tables and chairs, which he would sell to furniture makers. The shavings would just lie on the floor. Months would go by before Mrs. Reitter would sweep out the room. That was an event we children awaited with eager anticipation. We would peek into the room, and all you could see was smoke and dust. On hot summer nights, they moved their mattresses to the front of their room and sleep there amidst all the shavings. They were a filthy lot.

The largest and richest family were the Katzes. With their ten children, the Katzes lived in an apartment consisting of four rooms and a kitchen. Mr. Katz manufactured brooms and brushes right there in his home. He had regular benches, where workmen sat all day. It was a fun place to visit and play in; horse tails covered half-finished brooms and brushes. Loose hair flew and small children ran all over the place. The Katzes were well off and obviously on their way to great financial success, but their home was an unhealthy place to live in. All the Katzes had perpetual allergies, which the children in our neighborhood would tease them about.

Our family was industrious and closely knit, with everybody working and pooling their resources to maintain our home. We were determined to preserve our dignity and, at the same time, improve our lot. There was no sibling rivalry in our family; each of us was "our brother's keeper." We all started to work or begin an apprenticeship at the age of thirteen. My sister, Lenke, was a salesgirl in a large toy store in town. My brother, Moishe, worked in a large wholesale grocery store. Gershon entered into apprenticeship with a jeweler. My oldest sister, Piri, was a dressmaker and, at seventeen, converted our living–bedroom into a dressmaking salon. As the youngest, I was the "gofer" and everyone's pet.

Everyone worked for the common good of the family. Everyone, that is, except my sister, Kornelia, my father's

youngest daughter. She was two years old when her mother
died and was reared by her older sister. By the time my parents
married and she moved in with my mother, she was unmanage-
able. She was very pretty, but had what you would call learning
disabilities and was a bit of a juvenile delinquent. She was the
cause of a lot of family strife and made my mother's life a living
hell. She would tell tales to her older brothers and sisters and
they would come and argue with my mother. (In those days,
people were not aware of nor could they afford psychological
counseling.)

In my heart I knew that my mother was right. Still, no matter
whose side I took or whom I sympathized with, I would feel
guilty about the fact that I might be betraying someone. There
always seemed to be two camps vying for my loyalty. I often felt
like quoting Mercutio in Shakespeare's "Romeo and Juliet": "A
plague on both your houses!" There was such bitterness and
animosity among the two camps that it was not till forty years
after the war that my sister Lenke, on my mother's side, and my
brother Max, on my father's side—the only survivors besides
me—buried the hatchet. They were both in New York visiting
me! All through my life, I remained in the middle, retaining
close associations with both camps: my mother's out of love and
my father's out of respect and duty.

We all worked for a common goal, but no one worked harder
than my mother. She was the first to rise at dawn. She would
make the fire that lit the stove and have breakfast ready when
the rest of us woke up. We had no modern conveniences, no
radios, no dishwasher, no washing machine, no refrigerator or
ice box. We didn't even have any boxed or canned foods. All the
bread, cakes, challahs, and noodles we ate were made at home,
mainly by my mother. We preserved our own fruits and
vegetables in bottles. When we all left for work or school, my
mother would do the dishes. Then she would start making
lunch, our main meal of the day, which we ate at noon. We had a
two-hour break from either work or school, so we all walked
home for lunch. We always had soup as the main course and
some kind of dessert. My mother was not only a good cook, she
was a magician. She could make fresh vegetable soup three days
in a row and it would always be different. One day, she used
more potatoes so we had potato soup. The next day she added
fewer potatoes and added more peas, and we had pea soup. The
third day, she added more cauliflower and we had cauliflower

soup. Each soup had differently shaped, homemade noodles in it. My mother had a way with beans, potatoes, and noodles, the constant and cheapest available staple. We had potatoes mashed, fried, braised as a main dish or in a casserole, baked with eggs and cream. She made noodles from cooked riced potatoes and buttered bread crumbs, from grated raw potatoes smothered with cottage cheese. She served plain noodles of all shapes and sizes with meat, cheese, buttered cabbage or as a dessert with sugar and cinnamon or cocoa. Add to all this the home-baked bread and you know we never went hungry, but I am not so sure that we had all the necessary vitamins and minerals!

Besides her creative lunches, my mother had her other chores: washing, ironing, and mending clothes. I never saw my mother with idle hands, except on Shabbos and holidays.

She was a wonderful person, tall and pretty. She was very bright and had a lot of common sense. People said that she walked like a captain of the Hussars, the élite equestrian guard of the Hungarian army, the picture of both dignity and strength, commanding awe and respect. No matter where you threw her, she would always land on her feet. She was a deeply religious person, with firm orthodox convictions, devoted to Judaism in principle and in practice. Yet, she was very broadminded, tolerant of everyone with ideas and beliefs other than her own. She was the most kind-hearted, generous and charitable person I ever knew. I will tell you more about her generosity later.

Every Monday and Thursday were market days. The peasants and farmers from the outskirts of our town, some from as far as fifteen miles away, would gather in an open-air market that was many blocks long. They would start out in the middle of the night, some on foot, carrying their merchandise on their backs and their shoulders. Others came by horse-drawn wagon. Some came by train. They would line both sides of the street. Some would erect stalls; others would simply squat or sit and hawk their wares. You could buy a wagon load of wood or grain, or every kind of fruit or vegetable in season (by the pound or in bunches), as well as fresh eggs, butter, cheese, live chickens and ducks, geese and fish—in other words, everything that the farmers produced or gathered.

I loved to tag along with my mother to the market. While she shopped and bartered with the peasant women, other housewives would stop and ask my mother for her opinion:

"Mrs. Reisman, is this wood dry enough?" "Mrs. Reisman, is this fruit ripe enough?" She was an all-around maven, but particularly a certified poultry maven. She would take the chicken or goose, blow the feathers apart and, like a doctor, probe it with her fingers here and there. Then with great authority, she would give her verdict. Both the peasant women and our neighbors respected her judgment, and I was very proud of her.

My mother really earned the title of "poultry maven," and she traded on it. She always bought one or two geese, ducks or chickens to cut up and sell to other families. (There were kosher butchers, but they only sold very expensive beef or veal; the more affordable poultry had to be bought alive. Most people could not afford a whole goose and some did not want to bother with the routine of preparing the animal to eat. So, my mother became a middleman. That meant that we first had to shlep the poultry home. Then we had to take it to the *schochet*, the ritual slaughterer, to be killed. That task was usually delegated to the children. Thursday afternoon, you could see children, chicken or goose in hand, scurrying to and from the slaughterhouse. In those pre-television/pre-horror movie days, we got our thrills from watching a chicken thrash itself to death, then hang on a hook with its feet tied together. Often I became nauseated, but I had no time to dwell on the poor bird's fate, for I had to flick it. This had to be done by hand, while the chicken or goose was still warm; otherwise the feathers would not come out easily. We plucked the feathers in designated rooms, not very pretty places with chicken feathers flying all over. We saved these feathers and the goose down to make comforters and pillows.

The next step was to open the animal to take out the innards and clean it. Then the meat had to be koshered: first soaked in water and then every piece and every side of every piece had to be covered with salt. Next we separated the skin and fat. The fat was rendered and saved for cooking. In the rendering process, a tasty morsel called *grivenous* was left; this we sold together with the liver to a delicatessen store. We cut up the rest of the meat and sold it by the pound. The poorer people were, the less desirable the cuts they bought. Because my mother took on this job, we always had fat for cooking and meat for shabbos, which we could not otherwise afford. I became adept early on in life at opening and skinning a goose. I also delivered the orders. What I remember most is that I always delivered a piece of meat to a poor person who had not ordered it and could not pay for it.

I have told you that my mother was both a good cook and a magician. But it was really backbreaking toil, from dawn to midnight, that produced the delicious chicken soup, the roast goose, the homebaked challah and cakes, the noodles, the shining Kiddush cup and candlesticks, and the white tablecloth. But when she lit those candles and my father recited the Kiddush as we sat around that table dressed in our finery, it really seemed like magic.

Because my mother and everyone else in my family were always so busy, I, being the little one, sometimes got lost in the shuffle. I was everyone's pet, but no one person was in charge of me. Just as with a family pet, if no one is put in charge, one day everyone may feed it, and the next day it may go hungry. It may be overdisciplined or not disciplined at all.

My earliest memory goes back to when I was about three years old. I was sitting near a hot potbellied stove in Mrs. Rosner's house (which was a few doors away from ours), snuggled up in Mrs. Rosner's lap. She was telling me fascinating fairy-tales that I had never heard before. They were filled with princes and princesses, old witches and dragons. No one had ever read or told me a fairy-tale before. I knew I was supposed to go home, but I felt so cozy and happy that I wanted to hear more stories. When I finally left Mrs. Rosner's house, it was very dark outside. Afraid of the dark and the consequences of being away for a long time when nobody knew where I was, I ran home. Fearfully, I opened the door. No one knew I had been missing.

That evening was the beginning of a friendship with Mrs. Rosner that lasted throughout my childhood. In a courtyard full of poor people and characters, Mr. and Mrs. Rosner took the cake. They were rundown-at-the-heel, with no visible means of support. They were intellectuals who had fallen on hard times. They had one daughter, who was a school teacher somewhere in Prague, but she never visited them. Rumor had it that Mr. Rosner used to be a schoolteacher, who had been fired for some mysterious reason. His chief avocations were playing the violin, reading, and going to Kiddush. There were many *shuls* in town and he would visit all of them. By the time he came home, he was quite tipsy. But he would bring home from Kiddush whatever food he could stuff in his pockets.

The Rosners were shunned by most everyone, but I loved them. They became my mentors and opened a world of wonder to me that I never knew existed—the world of the Brothers Grimm, the world of make-believe.

They lived in one room and a kitchen. I don't know what they ate; I never saw Mrs. Rosner cook. She was just the opposite of my mother, who was always busy. Mrs. Rosner gave me her undivided attention. For years, on winter nights, I would sit on her lap and listen to her never-ending repertoire of fairy-tales. Mr. Rosner would play his violin or tell tales of faraway places he had visited or read about.

Mrs. Rosner awakened in me the love of nature. We would go on long walks through the woods or meadows that surrounded our town. I used to be chided by the other children, but I learned from the Rosners to march to the beat of my own drummer.

Another early memory from when I was about three or four years old: It is Friday night. I am in my grandparents' house. The house is filled with many people. They are all around the apartment and sitting two-deep around the table. People are sitting on the beds and we, the little ones, are sitting on top of an armoire, our legs dangling, looking down on people's heads. They are my aunts and uncles and cousins. (Our town was full of my relatives—businessmen and tradesmen, most more affluent then we. The custom was to gather on Friday nights after dinner at my grandfather's house; later, when he had died, we gathered at the oldest uncle's home.) I remember that it was a long walk to their house. I would hold my parents' hands and if there was a full moon, I'd follow it, as if sleepwalking. If there was no moon, I would close my eyes and daydream, imagining myself to be some character in one story or another. I did a lot of that as a child. I had no books or toys of any kind, so I had to develop and use my inner resources to amuse myself and occupy my mind.

We lived on a side street with no traffic and it was almost always teeming with children. The only thing we had in abundance was children, and they were all my friends. There were four of us who had been born on the same day and delivered by the same midwife. One of us was Clari, who was my best friend then and still is now. We had lots of fun. We played with makeshift dolls and beds fashioned out of boxes. We hammered four nails into empty spools of thread and weaved long strips from leftover wool. We would pool our pennies and maybe ten of us would chip in to buy a fifty-cent doll. Then we would sew dresses for it. We collected everything and anything and traded it. Flowers were a big item. The idea was to get every wild flower imaginable. This gave us an incentive to roam the meadows. Then we would press the flowers in old books. We also collected colored wrappers. We smoothed the wrappers till they were thin and made a rustling noise and then we pressed them.

We played all the group games children play everywhere, with balls and ropes, one group challenging the other. Some summer evenings a certain kind of flying beetle would invade the street. We would chase after the beetles with raised brooms and, after catching them, keep them in jars and trade them. While on the chase, we would sing a special song that went like this: "Czerebogar mikor lesz nyar, mikor as anyad gatyaba jar," a sort of Hungarian version of "Your mother wears army boots." The streets would reverberate late into the night with the laughter of children.

In the fall, we would climb the horse chestnut trees that lined our streets and pick the chestnuts. We would spend all afternoon removing them from the shells they had been growing in. We would pile the chestnuts one upon another and play a game similar to bowling, except that the winner got to keep the chestnuts he knocked down. There were days when I was a horse chestnut millionaire!

Early in life, we had learned to combine business with pleasure. The business of children was to run errands. We made these errands pleasurable by always stopping at a friend's home or two to get someone to accompany us. Besides the mundane errands like going to the stores, we took the challas, breads, and cakes to the baker, where we watched as they were placed in the gigantic ovens. We delivered messages from one part of the town to the other, because none of us had telephones. Some of us—Clari, for instance—had more interesting chores than others and so she was more fun to accompany. This was because her father had a fleet of hansom cabs, the private mode of transport at that time. When I was out with her, she would spot one of her father's hansom cab drivers, put the touch on him (cajole him into giving us some money) and then split it with me. The family also had cows, so Clari's chores included gathering potato peels and other vegetable discards to feed these animals. Clari's family knew such interesting people. One of their friends had a pastry shop and every time we stopped by, we would get to lick the bowls or be given the broken pieces of cake.

Sometimes we would get sidetracked from our errands by a "side show." A funeral, for instance, was good for an afternoon's entertainment. People in my hometown were not reserved; they gave vent to their emotions, happy or sad, and were fascinating to watch. The funeral procession would wind its way on foot, following a hearse drawn by a pair of splendid horses. The wailing and screaming of the bereaved family was accompanied by the steady murmur and repetitious chant of the faithful. Add to this the pomp and ceremony of the clergy in full regalia, the smell of incense, and you see why we were so fascinated. We would follow them to the cemetery, a favorite haunt of ours anyway. We'd get caught up in their grief, speculate about the life of the deceased, and try to satisfy our morbid curiosity. Or we would just reflect on the mysteries of life and death.

Sometimes there was too much horsing around, like the time I took my mother's *shaitel* (wig) to the wig maker to be combed out. The details of that trip are lost and forgotten, and so was the wig. I and my entourage ended up somewhere else, probably a funeral or some other side show, and the purpose of our trip slipped our minds, as did the wig. The next day my mother went to pick up the wig that wasn't. She was one wig poorer. As for me, well. . . the pain of that experience is long since forgotten.

Chapter 2

Small-Town School Days

As for my early school days, two things stand out most vividly in my mind: One is that I was often late because someone forgot to wake me up on time. The second is the most glaring disparity between the haves and the have-nots and the way they were treated in school. Nowhere else is the inequality of life more evident than in a small-town classroom.

I loved kindergarten. I was a quick learner and I loved everything about school. I loved the teachers, the songs we learned, the arts and crafts. I remember vividly the encouragement the teachers gave me, the kindness and fairness of the two teachers I had. But I also remember feeling betrayed by the false hope and promise they held out for me.

Like most six-year-olds, I entered school with great anticipations. I was eager to learn. It did not take me long to find out that the cards were stacked against me. All the Jewish children in our town attended the one Jewish day school we had. Our education was partially supported by the congregation and partially by the tuition our parents paid. Of course, with this being the only Jewish school in town, everyone had to be accepted. Rich or poor, we all went to the same school. But we were not treated equally. The rich kids sat in the front rows, and the poorer ones were relegated to the back. It was an accepted practice to butter up the poorly paid teachers with gifts, and it paid off handsomely. The greater your family wealth, the more favored treatment you received from the teacher. If you were poor, you did not have the means to curry favor. The teachers, knowing, as did everyone else, who the haves and have-nots were, perceived you as a non-entity.

Try to imagine this: Vulnerable and unprotected, you begin to notice the hole in your sweater and the one in your stockings; they have always been there, but now they begin to bother you. When the teacher asks questions, you always know the answers, but she does not call on you; she always calls on the first rows, and those kids don't know the answers, but she explains everything to them. Add to this the difference in homework and notebooks: theirs supervised and neat, yours unsupervised and messy.

Many times you are befriended by a rich kid and her parents. You are invited to come home with her after school so you could do homework together. They ply you with milk and cookies and chocolates that you don't get at home. You admire their homes and their clothes, but you can see that they are dumb. It takes them a long time to catch onto any new idea. You notice how much input their parents have, and how intimate their mothers are with the mostly spinster teachers. You are not surprised when they get better grades than you do. In spite of this, in the beginning my report card showed promise. But, eventually, given the circumstances, I gave up and simply began to coast.

The dictionary defines school as a place to acquire knowledge; it defines knowledge as experience, recognition, perception, enlightenment, glimpse, inkling, impression. My school gave me a glimpse of a society that I began to dislike. I did not find one teacher in the four years I was there eager to better someone's life. I found the class system of the middle European petite bourgeoisie oppressive, and I felt trapped.

It was 1936 or '37, I was about ten or eleven. My siblings were in their early twenties. Things were beginning to change for the better. My sister Piri married her childhood sweetheart and moved to a nice apartment of her own. She opened a larger salon, with a few girls working for her. She and her husband began talking about building a house on a lot that her husband had inherited from his grandfather. My brother Moishe, a very handsome man, also got married about the same time. His wife Alice was from Piestany, and as was the custom at the time, brought with her a large dowry, enabling them to open a grocery store. Suddenly we were not just respectable, there was evidence of real means of support. We remained a close-knit, sharing family. My mother continued to cook the main meals for everyone. There seemed to be enough money to make ends meet. There was a hint of promise of better times to come.

Lo and behold, one day we moved unexpectedly. It was only two streets away, but it was without a doubt an upward move. Four houses away from Piri, it was a private little house on a quiet side street. Besides us, only the landlord and one other

My sister Piri's wedding, 1937. I am sitting in front of the groom holding a bouquet of flowers. My mother is seated next to the bride. The older people in the front row are all her brothers and sisters with their spouses. The man seated on the right is the groom's father. Those standing are relatives of the groom and our cousins. Of all these people, seven survived; four died of natural causes; the remainder perished in the Holocaust.

family lived there. The apartment was just a little larger than our other home, but it had a foyer, with the kitchen to one side and two rooms to the other. One room was newly furnished with white furniture, the "in" thing of the time. This was the "young peoples'" room, which I shared with Lenke and Gershon. We had a flower garden and a white lilac tree, whose branches reached right into our window. The flower garden was not the only sign of our newfound gentility; the gates of our yard were locked, with only the tenants having a key. Best of all, we had our own toilet; it was still on the outside, but no one but our family used it, and my mother scrubbed it every Friday. What a stark contrast to our old home!

You would think I would be happy and content at this upward move. Well, I wasn't—not at the beginning, anyway. I missed my old familiar surroundings, my old friends and my old haunts. On a summer day that remains vivid in my memory, I left home early in the morning to visit my friends in my old house and didn't come home until evening. I visited first one friend and then another and did not notice that it had already gotten dark. Of course, we did not have a telephone, so my mother could not call anyone. Instead she came looking for me. Everywhere she went, they told her I had been there, but had already left. By the time I reached home, my mother had a praker in her hand. A praker was a flat, woven stick that was used primarily to beat the dust out of the carpets. Its secondary use was to intimidate and punish children. My mother introduced me to the praker that evening and afterwards I had great difficulty sitting down for days. I learned the lesson that my street urchin days were over.

Clockwise from upper left: My brother Moishe, my sister Piri, my niece and nephew, Malkele and Avrumele (taken in 1943), my brother Gershon.

Chapter 3

Better Times Before The Storm

Evidence of better times for us was everywhere. A new dress for my mother, a new suit for my father, plus gloves and scarves all mysteriously appeared. As our physical appearance improved, so did our meals. The chickens we slaughtered remained ours, the soups became thicker, there was butter on the bread. My mother was happy. She presided over a household that was prospering. Moishe's business took off and was doing well; Piri and her husband were building a new house. My sister Kornelia was married to a kind man and a good provider. Everyone was doing well. I, just at the threshold of my teens, was the greatest beneficiary of their good fortunes because they all sought to make my life easier and better than theirs had been. Little luxuries appeared. Lenke bought rollers to set my hair. She would bring board games for me. We would all play together and they would let me win. On Sunday, Lenke would not only take over my dishwashing chores, but would give me spending money and send me to the movies, which I loved. (She would cover up for me with my mother, who did not approve of the movies.)

Our winters were bitter cold. The river that divided our town would freeze early in December and remain frozen until March. It was frozen so solid that you could walk across it. Lenke would walk me to school on her way to work. Even in these, our more prosperous times, I was scantily dressed by today's standards. I had no boots, no slacks; just a thin coat, hat, and gloves. I remember forever being cold, my hands frozen and my feet wet. When we would get to the bridge we had to cross, Lenke, especially on cold windy mornings, would take off her scarf, wrap it around my face and head, and hold it there until we crossed the bridge. She found millions of ways to improve my life and I loved her and looked up to her. In fact, I worshipped the ground she walked on.

My schoolwork began to improve. Suddenly, there was hope. Lenke engaged one of my teachers to tutor me in "small Russian," the official language of Karpato-Ruthenia, our province. This was also the only language taught in the only "Teachers Academy." There was an unspoken understanding that if I did well, things could and would happen for me. If I did well, I could transfer into the Teachers Academy and then a good career in teaching or another profession would not be out of the question for me. I discovered that I had a good memory and an ear for foreign languages and that, if I applied myself, I could be a good student. And I was. Life continued to be beautiful.

I remember when I was about thirteen years old, my sister Kornelia made me a blue and red-flowered red crepe dress. Up until then, I always had dresses made by Piri, mostly from left-over fabrics, sometimes from more than one kind of fabric. Usually the style had to coincide with the availability of fabric. Often, my dresses were made over from old dresses. This was the first time I got to choose the fabric and the style. I chose a full-pleated skirt made of crepe. I was testing the Gods, waiting to see if it was really true that I could have a style that called for twice as much fabric. It was true. I even got a pair of matching red shoes! To me, this represented the height of luxury.

And then there was that magical Purim, when our lives were happy, carefree, and full of promise. Typically, in the early evening after all the *shalachmunus* (the traditional presents) were delivered, our family would sit down to the Purim *sudah*, always lovingly prepared by my mother. This year, more than ever before, our table was lavishly set, groaning under the delicacies that were not the usual fare for our family. My brother Gershon had borrowed a Victrola, and a record by Cantor Josele Rosenblatt played all through dinner. This was a first for us; the sweet music of Josele Rosenblatt proclaimed to us that all was well.

Purim was the only time we traditionally exchanged presents. Mostly they were edible goods: wine, cakes, and "exotic" fruits, like oranges and bananas. These, and all other tropical or semi-tropical fruits, had to be imported, so they were a great luxury that only the very rich could afford regularly. This year, Gershon, who was now a full-fledged jeweler and an accomplished engraver who was doing very well, began to shower us with an array of gifts: an engraved kiddush cup for my father, a shabbos knife with an ivory inlaid handle for my mother, and beautifully hand-engraved gold earrings for each of my sisters. Lenke still treasures hers, and every time I go to London to see her, she takes them out, together with old pictures and letters she saved from home, and we reminisce about that time of our lives, when life was good and hopes were high. She offers them to me, because she knows I would love to have them, but I cannot bear to take them from her. Those earrings singularly represent to me my family as it was then. They remind me of the closeness, the love, gratitude, respect, sharing, and all the things that are good in a closely knit family. When I look at those shiny earrings, they also remind me of the brief, shining moment in our lives when we were innocent, when we believed in tomorrow and forever after.

It was a time when my mother's kitchen was humming. Her trips to the market were more frequent and her baskets heavier. She always came home laden with goodies, heretofore unaffordable. My mother had always been a good cook and baker, but now our meals became more elaborate. There was more meat on the table, more chocolate in the babka. There was more wood in the shed and the house was warmer and more comfortable in the winter. My mother reminded me again of the Hussars, the equestrian elite of the Hungarian Army, who sat tall in their saddles with ramrod postures, dashing in their braided uniforms. Always the dignified "Hussar General," my mother now commanded a victorious army. There was a new spring in her walk, a new assurance in her voice as she bartered with the peasants. She also had occasional help in the kitchen, so there was time to relax. On languid, hot summer afternoons, we would go down to the river for a swim. My mother did not own a bathing suit; she would wear a cotton dress that billowed out like a big tent, and just float down the river. She was an excellent swimmer.

My mother ruled our house with an iron will, a tender hand, and a loving heart. Her actions were charitable, compassionate, and loving and they spoke louder than words. Almost no day went by that either an itinerant peddler, beggar or tinker did not find his way to our door and receive some leftover food, always kept handy by my mother. Quick to smile and to speak a kind word, my mother found other ways to share her bounty. There was a poor, bedridden old lady who lived at the edge of town with her niece, an old maid. They lived in one room. There were two beds, one of them always occupied by the old lady; an open cupboard; a small table; two chairs; and a chiffonier for clothes that had, instead of doors, a white embroidered cloth curtain. Despite the fact that they were dirt poor, that room was immaculate. The bed linens and the curtain were so white and starched that whenever I go to a fancy department store like Bloomingdale's, when they display a model bedroom with beautiful hand-embroidered linen, it always reminds me of that room. I would take food to the old lady and her niece: a bowl of soup, a piece of chicken, a challah for shabbos. My mother would also send a kerchief or a pair of stockings that my sisters had bought for her (secretly, of course, lest my sisters find out). When I protested that they were for her, she would say, "I can darn my old ones."

We had a cousin who fell on exceptionally hard times. His family had no money or food. They moved from the apartment they had occupied in better times to the edge of town, where they were surrounded by fields. They were proud people and only a handful of very close relatives knew of the severity of their plight. My mother was one of them. We would share some of our meals with them and I would always be the one to bring them food. One Sunday morning we had a heavy snowfall. My mother worried that they wouldn't be able to get out and would probably go hungry, so she sent me there with a container of food. Nothing fancy, just some delicious bean soup she had made. When I got to the gate, the yard was blanketed with virgin snow. No one had gone in or out. I plodded through the knee-high snow without boots, and when I reached the house, my cousin greeted me with great enthusiasm. I grumbled to my mother when I got home that it was unfair that I had to go there: "Why couldn't one of their children come out and get the food?" I complained. "They are all around my age." My mother answered, "Because, my child, the load is always easier for the giver than the receiver."

It was now 1938. Piri and her husband were expecting a baby; their new house was almost finished. Moishe had a beautiful baby boy and a thriving grocery store. He was very ambitious, a real entrepreneur. I adored him. I was his confidant, his sidekick, his slave. Every minute of my spare time I spent working in his grocery store. Then summer came and, wonder of wonders, I went to camp. This was the first real vacation of my life. It may not have been much by today's standards, but, to me, it was heaven. It was a Zionist youth camp. One of my cousins, a Zionist *macher*, pulled some strings, and there I was in the mountains with about two hundred boys and girls my age. Swimming in the river, hiking in the mountains, singing songs by the campfire. A certain red-haired boy noticed me. Those were carefree, sunlit days and nights. Who would think of reading the paper? We were oblivious to the distant thunder and dark clouds that were gathering, soon to engulf us all. That summer of 1938 was the first and last carefree summer of my teen-age years.

Chapter 4

The Beginning of the Storm

Hitler had ascended to power. Kristallnacht, the "Night of the Broken Glass," when a mass pogrom throughout Germany and Austria resulted in the destruction of scores of synagogues and thousands of Jewish homes and businesses; when 30,000 Jews were forced into concentration camps, heralded the near-extermination of the Jews. That date—November 9, 1938—is painfully etched in my memory. But, I was oblivious to it then. Germany seemed worlds away; if I did hear any talk of the persecution of Jews there, I do not remember hearing it. My earliest recollection that there was any danger to our lives goes back to that fall when I returned to school. I vividly recall sitting in the classroom, together with my fellow students and teachers, listening to the loudspeaker. We heard that our soldiers (the Czech Army) were poised on our borders with Germany, ready to defend our country. What I remember most about that day was a fear so overpowering, so foreboding, that it started in the pit of my stomach. It rose to become a noose around my neck that almost choked me. That lump, that fear, stayed with me for years and years, slowly growing bigger and bigger. I remember, years later, Eva saying to me, "Mother, don't say 'if' I grow old, say 'when' I grow old."

Did it ever really sink in that the threat to my life was over? I'm afraid that kind of fear does not go away. It lies there dormant, buried in your subconscious, to be conjured up every time you are uprooted. It surfaces regularly in nightmares, while you watch a movie, read a book, or even during casual conversation about the war. As years go by, it comes less frequently.

It will be fifty-two years this fall since that day in my classroom. I still remember that fear clearly; now it is something that has happened in the past. It lies buried under a blanket of security that Grandpa's love, devotion, and protection have woven. It is strengthened by the goodness of your Mommy and

Daddy and Eva's love and kindness, and by your sweetness, Jordan and Lauren. My many nieces and nephews and my loving relationship with them over the years have helped to weave that blanket of security, allay my fears and heal my wounds.

But back to history. I mentioned that I was sitting in my school classroom and heard the loudspeaker announce that Czech soldiers were poised on our borders, ready to defend our country. England and France, in order to appease Hitler, had allowed the Germans to annex Austria, and, on March 30, 1938, the German army had marched into Vienna. The history book, *Twentieth Century*, by Joseph Korbel, says that on that day, Hitler wrote, "It is my irrevocable decision to destroy Czechoslovakia by military means in the near future." He ordered his Army to prepare to take the Sudeten territory no later than October 1, 1938.

I remember that my classmates and I guessed about who would come to our aid first: the English, the French or the Russians. I personally put my trust in the Russians. After all, we were both Slavs. The gullibility and innocence of youth!

Meanwhile, a set of historic meetings revealed that neither France nor England would stand behind her obligation to protect Czechoslovakia. Instead of providing assistance, they provided Czech President Benes with an ultimatum: Accede to Hitler's demands or we will deny Czechoslovakia assistance and hold her responsible for the outbreak of war. Korbel's book notes that the ultimatum was presented to Benes at 2:30 A.M., that "the French envoy handing over his government's message wept" and the British envoy "looked persistently at the floor." On September 21, Benes and his government accepted the terms of the dictate. But that didn't satisfy Hitler. The next day, he made further demands, enraging British Prime Minister Neville Chamberlain, who then told Czechoslovakia that he could not "take the responsibility of advising Czechoslovakia not to mobilize."

And so, on September 23, Czechoslovakia mobilized. That was the day when we sat in our classroom listening to the loudspeaker.

War seemed imminent, but Chamberlain still could not see himself entering a war with Germany "because of a quarrel in a far-away country between people of which we knew nothing."

So, Chamberlain reached an agreement with Hitler, without a Czech representative's even being there. He appeased a power-hungry dictator by sacrificing Czechoslovakia—basically throwing her to the wolves. On September 30, betrayed by her allies, the Czech government was faced with the awesome choice of resisting alone or accepting what the other countries had decided for her. Czechoslovakia capitulated and the Germans annexed all of the Sudetenland, the westernmost part of our country. The most eastern part, where we lived, Karpato-Russia, was annexed by Hungary. The remaining part was divided into two separate entities: Czech and Slovakia. And so Czechoslovakia, as we knew it, ceased to exist. That marked the beginning of the end of my world.

Let me explain: Czechoslovakia had been the jewel of the East European countries. Before World War I, it had belonged to the Austria-Hungary monarchy, as most of Europe did, but after the fall of the Hapsburg Empire, a new, independent Czechoslovakia emerged. Czechoslovakia was then ethnically mixed. Besides the Czechs and the Slovaks, there were a wide variety of minorities. One such Hungarian minority, the Ruthenians, lived in our region. In addition, Germans comprised 22 percent of the population, with most of them living in the Sudeten, the western part of the country. While the Germans prospered in this heavily industrialized region, they retained their cultural heritage and remained politically and socially aligned with Germany and Austria.

Our new, independent Czechoslovakia was founded on democratic principles and lead by Thomas Masaryk, a professor from Charles University who was steeped in history, philosophy, sociology, political science, and literature—a Renaissance man. Above all, Masaryk was a humanist, with profound ethical and religious convictions. He was a man of worldwide reputation and respect, beloved by all. A far-sighted, sophisticated leader, he ruled with a gentle but sure hand. He was the father of our country, our own Washington and Roosevelt rolled into one.

Czechoslovakia stretched across Europe, touching Germany on the West, Poland, Hungary and Rumania on the East. Running down one length of the country was the majestic and un-penetrable Tatra and Carpathian Mountain chain. It was a modern land, lightly industrialized, inhabited by very liberal people. In sharp contrast, Hungary was a flat, agrarian country, ruled by a dictator named Horty Miklos who was fiercely anti-Slavic.

Hungary had had a slew of leaders towards the end of World War I, when the Hungarian nobility tried unsuccessfully to remain in power by establishing a monarchy. Refusing to compromise with other classes and nationalities, namely, the Russians and Ruthenians, the nobility left the door open to a succession of coups, some bloodless, others violent. Different factions held power for a while, but none succeeded in ruling for long or in uniting the diverse social classes and nationalities. Hungary was thus fertile ground for the Communist agitators, who had returned from the Russian prisoner-of-war camps. Their leader, Bela Kun, a native of Transylvania, had been totally indoctrinated while imprisoned in Russia. As Joseph Rothchild writes in his book, *East Central Europe Between the Two World Wars*, "Kun's Soviet government vaulted into office on a wave of national Bolshevik enthusiasm that transcended ideological lines."

Kun's overriding concerns were to establish a Marxist–Leninist society and to export his ideology to neighboring countries via military insurrection. His reign, however, was short-lived, too. The masses were quickly disillusioned by the persistent shortages. A right, radical backlash brought down his government. But the fact that a Communist government had managed to establish and maintain itself for 133 days in a country not geographically adjacent to Russia seemed to confirm that Communism was expanding. Therefore, at the end of World War I, the Treaty at Trianon punished Hungary for flirting with Bolshevism by stripping her of her natural borders, namely, the Carpathian mountains. In addition, Hungary was forced to curtail her army. That was why Horty, when he came to power, was so virulently anti-Slav and anti-Communist. Horty and his regime had their way of punishing the Communists, however. There were beatings, tortures and rapes. They executed five to six thousand victims, many of whom were Jewish. In addition, many outstanding members of the intelligentsia were driven into exile.

Meanwhile, the right radicals of the Horty cabinet were captivated by Germany's advances. In the spirit of ingratiation through imitation, they adopted German's anti-Semitic laws.

They were rewarded on November 2, 1938 with annexation of our territory—my home!

And so, with the stroke of a pen, we were to become Hungarians. I remember that my father quipped at the time, "If the Czechs would march out and the Hungarians would not march in, the Jews would be all right." But in they marched. And we were there to "welcome" them.

Our town was the capital city of the region and it housed both the municipal and the military headquarters. At the outskirts of the town stood a large military garrison. While citizens young and old stood watching, crying and cheering, one army marched out and the other marched in. Both were, by today's standards, unsophisticated, mostly horse-powered armies, with few mechanized vehicles. The Czech army, better equipped than the Hungarian army, had all its armored vehicles stationed at the border, where the soldiers fully expected to fight the Germans. But the Czech soldiers were defeated before they could prove themselves. Some showed their grief, others sang. And we, the people, bewildered and afraid to show emotion, cried inwardly as we cheered for them. I remember standing there with my father, who had a long red beard. One soldier jumped out of the lines, pointed to his beard, and said, "Old man, the Hungarians will make you cut off your beard." Those were prophetic words.

No sooner did the echo of the footsteps of the last Czech soldier die out than we could hear, from another direction, the approach of the jubilant Hungarian army. Their leader had aligned himself with Hitler and we were the first prize. The whole town, young and old alike, was sent out to greet them, cheering the victors. We were apprehensive, afraid of the future, but each of us was eager to assure ourselves and our neighbors that we meant to be patriotic Hungarians.

At first, life went on as usual without much change. Hungarian became the official language, but we were all bilingual so that created no problem—except in school. Before this restructuring, the Czechs and Hungarians had been mortal enemies, so we had been forbidden to speak Hungarian in school. Now it was the reverse: I was forbidden to speak Czech in school. I had been educated in the Czech language. I spoke it fluently and correctly. I read all the European classics—Fyodor Dostoevsky, Victor Hugo, Charles Dickens—in Czech. By the same token, my mother had grown up in a town that was part of the Austro-

Hungarian Monarchy; her generation spoke Hungarian and it became my mother tongue as well. (Only the "intelligentsia" spoke German.) Since the language at school had been Czech, Hungarian was really just our "kitchen" language; I had never learned the correct grammar, making school a newly difficult experience.

The change in language was just the beginning. With the new school year came new "rules": Jewish children were to be dismissed from all schools of higher learning, including gymnasium and business schools. That meant that our public school education had to end at the ninth-grade level.

There was, however, the privately run "Hebrew Gymnasium." Housed in a brand new, beautiful building, it had an excellent teaching staff and curriculum. Unfortunately, it was also very expensive, attended only by the affluent, modern Jews. My father, an impoverished "Melamed" (teacher) was neither, so the elitist Hebrew gymnasium was out of my reach. Knowing this, I lost interest in school as it had become a dead end for me.

The new borders between us and Hungary, however, created new business opportunities that my entrepreneur brother, Moishe, quickly seized upon. While I tended the store, he traveled to the Hungarian heartland, exporting chocolates and importing smoked goose, a delicacy unknown to us. The idea was to expand and we did. Moishe made contact with a pharmaceutical firm and contracted to supply them with medicinal flowers and herbs. I have very pleasant memories of spending the summer of 1939 climbing trees and combing the meadows for indigenous flowers and herbs, which we dried and shipped out at a great profit. I also remember buying up all the blueberries in town for blueberry brandy. Oh, Moishe was brimming with ideas, but the powers that be had ideas of their own! That same year, they took Moishe's business out from under him.

How did this happen? Anti-Semitism. There was always covert anti-Semitism. Jews were different; they did not believe in Christ and, were therefore, at best, tolerated. The Jew was industrious; he had business acumen and was successful. So, Jews were begrudgingly respected but, at the same time, envied and hated.

Suddenly, the Hungarian regime allowed anti-Semitism to flourish openly and the long-suppressed envy and hatred were allowed to rise to the surface; in fact, the government encouraged it. The Jew was not to be trusted. Overnight, he became a "warmonger," a "callous moneylender," an "abuser"—whatever description was needed to ease the consciences of the gentiles when they took away Jewish property.

Most of the Jewish businesses had their licenses revoked and transferred to Gentiles. Officially, the new arrangement was called a partnership. It was said that the Jew, who could no longer be trusted, needed the guidance of a Gentile. Unofficially, this meant that, after a few weeks or a month, when the new Gentile "partner" learned the business, the Jewish "partner" was kicked out. Only those Jewish businessmen with very large concerns that were difficult to operate remained as "partners" in their own establishments.

Still, in that utter gloom, there was a glimmer of hope: Lenke emigrated to England in the spring of 1939, with the promise that Gershon and I would follow her. In the meanwhile, she planned to support us royally by sending us her salary from London. (The English pound was then the most valuable currency.) Lenke did send money for awhile. But then, at the end of that year, the Hungarian government closed its borders to the West and all communication came to an end.

Watching my personal world unravel around me, and filled with the sense of the hopelessness of my life as a student, I quit school that year at the age of fourteen. For a while, I worked in a paper-bag factory, sealing the bags with my fingers, which bled every night. After a few months of that, my family decided that, rather than have me earn the few pennies I did, I should learn dressmaking. There were two ways of doing that: one, to pay someone for six months or a year to give me an intensive dressmaking and patternmaking course and then get a certificate and a job in a fancy salon. (These were springing up all over because, as in every war, there were profiteers and people with money, with no ready-to-wear industry to sell them clothes). The second way, which I was forced to choose, was to apprentice for three years and move along much more slowly. When I started out, my major responsibility was to sweep the workshop and run errands. By the time those who could afford the better apprenticeships were earning money, I was still running errands and sewing buttons. I was not included in the patternmaking classes, had no certificate, and was not earning any money from dressmaking.

Then came the spring of 1940, when the Hungarian military service began to systematically draft Jewish men for labor camps. At first, they took only those who were eligible for the military. Then older men began to be drafted for a few months at a time. When Hitler and his allies began to lose the war, every Jewish male up to the age of 45 was put in forced labor camps.

While working in Hungary, the men built roads and did other menial jobs. Most of them, however, were sent to the war zones, especially to the Russian front. There the Hungarian Army joined the German and Italian armies on their march toward Moscow. The Jewish men were used as cannon fodder—always in front of the advancing armies, digging ditches and carrying weapons for the soldiers.

Grandpa and my brother Moishe ended up in Russia, Moishe never to be heard from again. Gershon, in order to avoid the draft, secretly took a train to the Polish border one summer afternoon, and crossed into Poland illegally. His plan was to fly from there to London, but when the Germans bombed Krakow, Poland and thus unleashed the horror of World War II, he fled together with many others from the advancing German Army to the Ukraine. The Ukraine is a constituent republic of the Soviet Union, rich in agriculture. When we heard from Gershon (we heard from him twice), we learned that he was working on a "Collective Farm." Later the Germans invaded that region, too, and he must have fled again and disappeared to somewhere in Russia. With Gershon and Lenke gone, the heart and soul of our house were killed.

The slow strangulation and disintegration of our family, as well as the ultimate destruction of the Hungarian Jews, had begun. At home, the noose was tightening. Moishe's wife, Alice, who by now had two beautiful children, was totally helpless and unable to cope. She had first lost contact with her family members when Czechoslovakia was divided, since they remained on the Czech side. Later in the war, they were taken to concentration camps, where none survived. With her husband gone, Alice, who had been raised in luxury, was now totally dependent on us, and we were in sad shape. To this day, I do not know who paid her rent. I know that she moved with her exquisite furniture to the "wrong" side of town and I became her liaison to the world. She and her children ate with us often and my mother would shop and cook for her. I would trek there at night to bring her the food and would sleep with her and the children. For years and years after the war, I had nightmares in which children were crying because they were hungry and I had abandoned them. They would say, "You did not come today," and I would plead, "But I don't know where you are." Then I would wake up in a cold sweat.

I didn't need a psychiatrist to interpret these endlessly recurring dreams.

And then, sweet Jordan, you were born. How does one explain a grandmother's feelings when she looks at her first grandchild for the first time? Wonder. Elation. The purest of joys! There is this little life, your flesh and blood. There is at once this promise of immortality, a new generation that links you to the future and, at the same time, allows the possibility of reaching back into the past.

We named this baby "Jordan Michael"—in Hebrew, Joseph Moishe—after my beloved brother Moishe. Joseph Moishe had been his full name. My only son was named after my father, so here, finally was my chance to perpetuate the name of my long lost and cherished brother, a chance to reach back into the past.

Your arrival, Jordan, also acted as a catalyst for me in dealing with the demons inside me. When I cradled you in my arms, it was an affirmation of life, accompanied by a totally secure feeling of hope and of faith in the future. This security allowed me to finally face and accept the loss of those innocent young lives. With my grandchild safely in my arms, I could mourn my dead family and lay them to rest.

At the same time, with my grandchild as my shield, I was able to face my feelings of guilt for not having been being able to save those children who had died. I was like the young boy in the movie, "Ordinary People," who blamed himself for the accidental drowning of his brother. In the end, he realized that he could not have saved his brother; his only crime was that he had held onto the boat when his brother could not.

I totally identified with that boy who survived. I, too, am beginning to realize that my only crime was that I also held onto the boat while others could not. But once I witnessed the birth of my grandchild, the affirmation that our family had a future—I could let go of my demons and my nightmares stopped.

You may wonder why the birth of your Dad and Eva did not heal my pain the way your birth did. This was because, when they were born, right after the war, I was still in shock. In order to survive I could not let all the hurt and pain come to the surface and so it lingered in my subconscious. Only when my life regained some kind of stability and tranquility and I could live for some time among people who were leading normal lives could I allow the enormity of my loss to hit me.

When I first saw you in the hospital, looking so beautiful and energetic, so full of life, I promised myself that I wouldn't let anything or anyone harm you. The next day I came back to the hospital and there you lay, lethargic and listless under the lamp, yellow with jaundice. My heart sank. I was devastated, crushed by my total helplessness. I thought of my mother. She was a grandmother, her grandchildren as precious to her as you were to me. Suddenly, I comprehended the horror she must have felt in those final moments when she saw she could not protect us. For months after that, every time I held you, I thought of all those little ones I had loved, of those grandmothers and mothers that were lost, and I cried.

Let's return to our history. It is late 1940. Piri and her husband, together with their two small children, have been in their new house for about two years. Her husband has been reveling in his independence. Finally, they were on their own. This very private man had been enjoying being the head of his household, the sole provider, with his wife having the luxury of being only a mother and homemaker. His enjoyment, however, was short-lived. Very soon he was saddled with a whole family because my mother, father and I were forced to move in. He had built a small bungalow in his backyard, consisting of a foyer, a room, and a small kitchen and we lived there. Soon it did not matter, though, because he was away most of the time in the labor camp and Piri was forced to go back to dressmaking. In addition, she rented one room to a Jewish woman whose husband was in Russia and who could no longer afford her home. This woman took her meals wit us. Once again my mother did the cooking for everyone.

Our bungalow was unheated and we would place warmed bricks in our beds in order to sleep. By morning, the water in the washbasin would be frozen. My father, always a frail man, started to cough. By the next summer, he was wasting away.

Because of the war, there were food shortages that summer, including an acute shortage of bread. The new wheat was yet to be harvested and the old supply was running low. The bakeries were given flour rations, but not enough to go around. So long lines formed in the middle of the night, while the bread baked. Anyone in the back of the line had a good chance of coming home empty-handed. This was a mild catastrophe, since bread was such an important staple. During the two or three weeks of the shortage, it was my job to bring home the bread for all of us. My father was getting weaker and had lost his appetite. He had trouble swallowing, and longed only for a fresh roll and butter. Rumor had it that there was only one bakery that had rolls. It was the largest one, owned by a Nazi with the right connections. I got up at four in the morning to stand on line. There was one for the Jews and one for the Gentiles. Four Gentiles were let in for every Jew. I saw that the supply of rolls was getting low and the Jewish line was not moving. I jumped into the Gentile line. No one paid any attention to me until I had the rolls in my hand and the owner recognized me. He said, "She is a Jew and was on the wrong line. Don't give her the rolls." I started to cry and scream that my father was sick and wanted a roll. I got the sympathy of the crowd and they yelled back, "O.K. Give them to her." Reluctantly, he gave me the rolls.

I felt two great satisfactions from that incident: one, my father enjoyed the rolls, and two, that Nazis had to stand in a bread line in Siberia! How did that happen? When the Russians liberated us former Czechoslovakian citizens, they did not look upon us as "the enemy." The Czechs never collaborated with the Germans; in fact, there was a free Czech army fighting alongside the Russians, even as the country was occupied by the Germans. But there were some Nazi collaborators and the Russians had a long list with their names on it. These collaborators were mercilessly rounded up and shipped to Siberia. I told one Russian Jewish soldier what happened with the rolls for my father and he saw to it that that Nazi went to Siberia!

My father died that fall of 1941. The whole town turned out at his funeral to praise and honor him; the chief Rabbi delivered a long-winded eulogy about his contribution and devotion to the children. Again, long on honors, but short on cash. While my father was ailing, the Jewish congregation that ran the Chader where he taught stopped all payments to him. So my father's estate consisted of a good name, lots of honors, a few well-worn suits, some pairs of shoes, and a set of *tefilin* that my mother sold. I do not recall my that mother ever cried or carried on as much, before or after, as she did when we sold his shoes and *tefilin* .

I was seventeen when my father died and had no way of earning money. I hadn't yet completed my dressmaking apprenticeship. My mother had a bad back and was laid up all that fall and winter. Piri took care of her and the children. Drastic measures were necessary, so I took a leave of absence from my apprenticeship and, following in my mother's footsteps, I turned to the geese. I had to work on a larger scale because many people were depending on me. One of my cousins bankrolled me. I arranged with a few peasant women that every Wednesday they would bring whatever poultry they had to my home and I would buy it from them. This way, they had a sure buyer and I was assured a steady supply. I would buy up to fifteen or twenty chickens and geese every week. I also arranged for the *schochet* to come on Thursdays and slaughter them in our yard. (I was not the only chicken running around without a head.) With Piri's help, I plucked and cleaned them and sold them to eager buyers. To the elite, I hand-delivered whole geese. They paid well for this service. The rest I opened up, rendered, made kosher, and sold by the kilo to people who came in a steady stream from Thursday afternoon late into the night.

We seldom had anything left beyond what we needed or gave away to the very poor. In this way, we made it through the winter. We ate well; we were warm. There was even one fringe benefit: I sold the feathers and the goose down to a quilt maker and my mother told me that that was my money to do with as I wanted. I bought some wool tweed fabric and had my very first custom-made coat. It was beautiful and I felt good all over.

Since we were so close to the Slovakian border, a stream of Slovak Jews silently passed through our town, as they, for a fee, were being smuggled out to escape the German occupiers, who were systematically deporting Jews. Some stayed in our town. One old couple rented our kitchen and another wealthy young man, our bedroom. They hoped to wait out the war in our home unnoticed, which they did. Being there illegally, of course, they paid well for this privilege. It was a mutually beneficial arrangement because, while it enabled these people to survive, it also assured our financial survival. My mother and I, however, felt totally displaced. We had even rented out our beds, and were sleeping in those vacated by members of our family who had been sent to the labor camps. But our independence had already been taken from us when that happened.

I was getting restless. I saw no future for me, with or without the war's end; and the end was nowhere in sight. In the winter of 1942, an opportunity presented itself; , with Piri's and my mother's consent, I grabbed it. A wealthy grain merchant, who, according to our friends, had impeccable credentials, was seeking a mother's helper for his wife and three small sons, who were her stepchildren. His wife was a lovely lady, much older than I, who had a hard time coping with the house and these three unruly boys. Their mother had died and she was a stepmother they did not want. My duties turned out to be much more than I had bargained for, but I did not mind work and I got along well with her and the boys. I was well received by their extended family and I was happy. Unfortunately, I was too naive to recognize signs that the man of the house was often too close to me. A few months passed and the lady of the house went to a nearby village to visit her parents. She took the two smaller boys with her and left the older one with me. In the morning, the husband went off to work, taking the boy with him to drop him off at school. About noon, he returned unexpectedly and began to chase me through the house. I finally managed to lock myself in a room. After awhile, he left. I packed my bags, walked to the railway station, and went home. Arriving unexpectedly, I told my mother that the lady of the house had left for a few days and that I had to come home. She never questioned my decision; she simply said, "I am sure that you had a good reason." A few days later, I got a postcard from the lady, expressing her indignation that I would leave without giving her notice after she had been so kind to me. My mother read the postcard after I did and asked, "Do you want to answer it or shall I throw it away?" I said, "Throw it away" and we never discussed that matter again. I hesitated to write about this now, but I had to show you what a wonderful person my mother was and what a great relationship we had. We were generations apart and any discussion of sex was taboo, but she trusted me and my judgment in these matters implicitly and said so with her actions. I remember well the talks we had as she walked me to the railway station when I was leaving town to be a mother's helper and when I left for Budapest for a new job opportunity. I remember her telling me during one of these talks that if she could, she would give me the world, but she knew she could not. She said she knew that her world was crumbling and that mine might be in danger. She understood that I had to find my own way and whatever might be good for me was right for her. I think that is the greatest gift a parent can give to her child.

Home once again, I settled down to a life of quiet desperation. Together, we learned to live with each setback, Looking back at that time, what amazes me most is the adaptability of the human spirit. Despite our situation, if you think that my friends and I were always sad and dejected, you are wrong. We were not unlike teenagers everywhere. We went to the movies, to social dances; we sang and we laughed. I fell in love. It did not last and I thought I would die, but I got over it. All the normal growing pains were there. Its just that also present underneath it all was the quiet, grinding hopelessness.

In the winter of 1943, I struck out once more for independence. With my mother's blessing, and armed with jars of homemade roux (the base for soups), rendered goose fat, and other homemade goodies, I decided to try my luck in Budapest, miles from home. This was a major step in those days for a girl of not quite eighteen. In retrospect, I wonder where I got the

guts. I rented a room the size of a closet from the sister of one of our friends. The first day I arrived, I went to visit a very wealthy cousin of mine, who lived in the most fashionable part of town. She showed me her wardrobe of fashionable, custom-made clothes. During our conversation, she mentioned the address of her dressmaker. On the way home, I stopped by that dressmaker's salon, dropped my cousin's name (without her permission, of course) and, by stretching the truth a lot, I got a job there. I was very lucky.

The author at age 17.

The owner was a very kind and compassionate person. She saw through my naiveté and inexperience, but did not take advantage of it. While my skills were inadequate, my determination to succeed was great. She and the others in that elegant, high-fashion establishment patiently taught me and guided me. I became their adopted "country bumpkin" and I earned a living wage. I traded my mother's rendered chicken fat for other staples and I cooked for myself. I ate meat only when my mother sent it to me with someone from our hometown who was visiting Budapest. I joined a Zionist youth movement, where I met other young people with similar backgrounds. They, too, had come to the big city to make a new life for themselves. But that was not to be, for suddenly, in March, 1944, our hopes were dashed. Out of the blue, one Friday morning, the Germans invaded Budapest.

Within a few hours of the German army's arrival, soldiers were stationed at all the railway stations, arresting every Jew arriving or leaving Budapest. The same was true for every bus and railway station in every town. All the escape routes were sealed off. Of course, I was determined to get home. My friends and I went to the railway station and observed the situation; we all agreed that the sooner I left, the better. I remember looking in the mirror and saying to myself, "No one knows me here and I am not Jewish." I struck up a conversation with a young Hungarian soldier, who was going to my hometown for the first time to be stationed in the military barracks. I promised to be his guide. Deep in conversation, we passed the German sentry. By the time we reached home, every one in the train assumed that I was with him, so I was not asked to present any I.D. cards, which, of course, I didn't have. I watched with suppressed horror as a czendor (the Hungarian equivalent of an American state trooper) led away two Jewish men who had been on our train. The czendor's, in their braided uniforms and tall feathered hats were élite and imposing figures who by their very presence were threatening and intimidating to everyone, especially Jews.

To further insure my safety, I proposed to the Hungarian soldier that we share a hansom cab. I am sure that that bashful young man could not figure out why I found him so fascinating, nor why I clung to his every word. The truth was that I was scared to death and did not dare take my eyes off him.

And so I arrived home with the news that the Germans had occupied Budapest.

One Friday morning, German pilots in painted planes staged a mock air raid over Budapest. Under the pretext of coming to aid, they invaded Hungary and immediately set out to make it *Juden-Frei* ("Jew clean"). What they meant to do (and almost succeeded in doing) was to get rid of the Jews in Germany and then exterminate all the Jews of Europe. One poster hanging in an exhibit in Budapest said it all. It had been posted after all the Jews in our town had been deported. Dated May 24, 1944, it read: "All signs which are reminders of Jews are to be removed within three days. This order should be considered everybody's patriotic duty."

The Germans moved quickly and efficiently. Only four or five truckloads of soldiers came into our town, but this was enough to take complete control. New edicts, appearing overnight on lampposts, were issued daily: Every Jew, including children, must wear the Yellow Star of David. All Jews must abandon their places of business, jobs or, if professional, their affiliations to all institutions. A five o'clock curfew was established and we were not allowed to leave the city limits. An offender was immediately taken to the Ghetto.

Typically, a Jewish "ghetto," like the most famous one in Venice, which dated back to the sixteenth century, was a Jewish quarter comprised of a few streets close together in the center of town, where all Jews were required to live. Often, this was ordered by the local government for easy surveillance of the Jews, though sometimes the ghetto was self imposed for protection and security. When the Germans occupied towns like Budapest or Warsaw and wanted to segregate the Jews, all they had to do was to cordon off the streets in the Jewish quarter and bring in the Jews from the rest of the city. Then they had a ready-made ghetto. Jewish families lived there for years.

We had no such Jewish quarter. The Jews, comprising over one-third of the population of our town, were scattered all over, in secure and mostly harmonious relations with their neighbors. So when the Germans occupied our town, their first task was to create a ghetto in a hurry. The purpose was twofold: first, to immediately separate Jews from their possessions; second, to get them into a concentrated place.

Amidst open fields was a sprawling brickyard (factory),

which belonged to the Moskowitz family, the richest Jews in town. It consisted of many buildings with giant kilns, where the bricks were fired, and with acres and acres of open-sided lean-tos. They surrounded the place with barbed wires and watchtowers and the feared "czendors" gendarmes stood guard. Within three weeks, they marched into the buildings 18,000 Jews from out of town and the vicinity—literally herded them like animals into a corral, without any resistance from the Jews whatsoever. Into this building marched the young and old, the rich and poor, the sick and the able, newborn infants and feeble old people, with only the possessions they could carry. They had even emptied the hospitals and the asylums.

The people huddled there in despair and discomfort. I cannot describe the conditions inside that ghetto because, by some unexplained quirk of fate, I was spared. I could ask my friends who were there, but that demon I cannot face.

I know that in this ghetto, the people spent three rainy, windy April weeks; from there they were taken by cattle cars to Auschwitz. Upon their arrival, my mother, my sister Piri, my sister-in-law Alice and their four children were stripped naked, had their hair shorn, and then led to the gas chambers. They were killed there together with all the town's children and all the older people. Only those men and women over sixteen or seventeen years of age and under about forty-five, who were able-bodied and did not hold onto a child, were spared. They were put into concentration camps, where they performed slave labor and were slowly starved to death.

It is difficult to describe those last few days I spent at home. We were all paralyzed with fear, helplessly, hopelessly caught. I remember I felt as if someone had put a noose around my neck and, with each passing day, was tightening it. The Jewish leaders cautioned us not to antagonize the Germans. They felt that if we were meek and submissive, the Germans would be lenient with us. I did not agree with this then and I blame them for it now. To me, it is unforgivable that a leadership of an affluent society, such as the Hungarian Jews were, did not use some of its resources to find out what was happening while the Jewish world was burning around us, and prepare to organize for the eventuality that this could happen here. Instead of submissive weakness, avenues of escape should have been prepared.

I vowed that I would not be led alive anywhere. I would rather take my own life. Perhaps because of that, or because her children were scattered—or because I was the only unattached apple of her eye—or simply because she was a courageous and independent woman, my mother became obsessed with saving me.

Chapter 5

My Escape

Lekard was a border village, eight kilometers from us. It divided Hungary from Czechoslovakia. From that village came a man who was a smuggler. With the help of my cousin, who was a Zionist leader more courageous than most, he organized a number of successful escape parties. About twenty Jews would gather during the day in a house on the outskirts of town. About midnight—for a large fee, of course—the smuggler would lead them to Czechoslovakia. It was like jumping from the frying pan into the fire, because the Germans were there too, but there was an active Czech underground that was also trying to help and we were, at least, buying time.

My mother arranged for me to go on one of those trips. Amidst sad good-byes, I remember holding my neck because I felt as if I were choking. That night, at about eight o'clock, my sister, ignoring the curfew, came to the gathering house and told me that my mother had fainted and was very distraught and that I had to come back. When I got home, my mother was sitting on a low bench. She had just found out what I had known in my heart for a long time—that my brother Moishe was killed in Russia. She took me on her lap and asked me to forgive her, but she could not let me go. Amid tears, she assured me not to worry, and that God would not let harm come to us.

God did not hear. The next day, the curfew started at eight in the morning, and at nine, they started gathering the Jews from the far end of town into the Ghetto.

The last few days, our Gentile neighbors rose to the occasion: they saw an opportunity and grabbed it. They ran to Jewish neighbors and asked for our valuables—jewels, linens, silver, etc.—to save for us until we returned. (Few returned, and those that did recovered very little.) About noon that day, out of the blue, a peasant boy of about twenty years of age walked into our home. My mother and my sister-in-law were sitting in one corner, grieving for my brother; the bundles that we were sup-

posed to take with us were in the middle of the floor. There were
also pails of hard-boiled eggs; the children were running around
unrestricted, playing ball with the eggs. My mother's precious
compotes, saved from year to year to be used for special oc-
casions, were being thrown around by the children. The peasant
boy told us that he was Misha, brother of Maria Cuprinka, and
that his mother had sent him to ask if we had anything of value
to hide. I was for throwing him out immediately, and told him
so in no uncertain terms; but he paid no attention to me. My
mother started with her tale of woe, telling him that she had
nothing of intrinsic value, only her children and that she was
losing them one by one. She told him what happened the night
before and how I could have been saved. It happened that the
Cuprinkas also lived in Lekard and Misha knew the smuggler.
Misha stared at us in disbelief as my mother spoke. Late in the
afternoon, he went out into the street. From where he stood, he
could see the column of silent old men, women, and children
with their bundles in their hands walking into the Ghetto. Misha
watched that sickening scene, came back to our house, stared at
me, and then, all of a sudden, announced that he would take me
with him. He would hand me over to the smuggler or put me over
the border himself. This time, I refused to go. But, as night fell, I
was pushed out of the house without even a good-bye. As I was
leaving, a pious old man, who lived with us recited loudly,
"Yvorechech Hashem Veyishmorecho. . ." "May the Lord bless you
and keep you; may the Lord shine His countenance upon you. . . ."
At the time, the meaning of this prayer was unknown to me. Yet
when I was in the greatest danger, I took solace in those words.

Misha led me to his bicycle. I tore off my Star of David and
we rode through the deserted streets, our hearts pounding.
When we finally reached the open roads, surrounded by fields,
we could see the searchlights of the Ghetto in the distance. We
took turns riding and walking. As we walked, we held hands to
keep each other from shaking. In one village, we were stopped
by a patrol. Misha explained that he and his "sister" had been
detained in the city. I realized then that I should find out something about the Cuprinka family. I kept repeating the informa-
tion Misha gave me—such as the dates of birth of his family—so
that I would not be found failing. As we reached his house, we
heard another patrol yell "HALT!" Instinctively, though Misha
had never seen a movie, he pushed me against the wall and put

his arms around me. When the patrol aimed their searchlight at us, they thought we were a couple of lovers and left. Then Misha led me into his home and pushed me in front of his mother. All the pent up emotions of the last few days spilled out and I burst into uncontrollable tears. The Crupinkas were deeply religious people who truly believed that I had been sent to them by the Virgin Mary—not only to save my life, but to save my soul.

The next morning, the village was buzzing with the news that Wednesday night, a group of Jews, led by one of the villagers, was caught crossing the border. The Cuprinkas realized then that they had a hot potato on their hands. There was no one to turn me over to. They could not put me over the border themselves because of the tightening of the patrols. So they decided to keep me with them. It was a decision, I am sure, they regretted many times. Unless they turned me over voluntarily, they were in just as much danger as I; my safety became theirs. In the middle of a March night in 1944, they took me to the edge of the field and placed me in an enclosed hayloft. I lay there in a stupor and slept for the next three days.

One day, their half-witted servant, Jan, stumbled over me. It was explained to him that I was an orphan and that some bad men wanted to kill me. He was an orphan, too. He became my protector, later my roommate. He saw to it that, like the animals he cared for, I was fed before he left to work in the fields. Misha realized that, just as Jan had found me, anyone else could, since there was no lock on the door. To install one would arouse suspicion. And so we designed the first of our inventions: he placed four benches on the hayloft floor, covered them with lumber, and then piled on the hay. He made a huge haystack with enough room on the bottom, under the benches, for one person to lie down. On one side, he tied the hay into a bale; by pulling it out, it became a door. There I lay, fully clothed, for five long weeks.

For five days after I arrived, the Cuprinkas took turns visiting my home, bringing with them fresh milk, bread, and cheese. They brought back from my home and the homes of my relatives everything of value that could be taken out without arousing too much suspicion. This was considered payment for my safety. They told me that my mother was a changed person since I left. The thought of my safety had given her new courage. She was once again calm and self-controlled.

My sister had an elegant overnight case, one of her treasured possessions. My mother filled it with a toothbrush, a nightgown, a long robe, a change of underwear and five books that I happened to have around the house. It was a "regulations survival kit"—or maybe she wanted to imagine that I was spending a weekend in a resort. Escape from reality was a necessary in retaining some measure of sanity!

I had my own "escape routes." I would weave tales in which I was always the central character—the prettiest, richest or most famous. I would tell myself stories that would last for days. This way, in the morning, when I awoke and asked myself where I was, the answer would not be a flea-bitten barn, but on a ride through the woods or on a picnic at the seashore. I would continue the story from where I had left it the day before. Meanwhile, the Cuprinkas, together with many peasants from the surrounding villages, brought free milk and produce to the Ghetto. One evening, when Misha brought me supper, he stared at me with a mournful look—the same one I had seen on that fateful day when I had left my home with him, I knew without a word that it was all over. My family was gone, probably to a labor camp.

Despite the stories I told myself, those first few weeks in the haystack were the worst. I thought I would lose my mind and I sincerely considered going into the Ghetto. The Cuprinkas pleaded with me not to. They knew that if I were caught, their lives would be endangered. To keep me occupied, Misha took a deep iron drawer that was used in the stove to catch ashes, stole some thick candles from the Church, stood the drawer up, placed the candles inside, and created a reading room for me in the middle of the haystack! I know that *Gone With the Wind* is one of the most widely read books in the world, but I think I can safely say that I hold the distinction of being the only person to have read it inside a haystack, by candlelight, time and time again.

It rained a lot that April. Although the rain meant safety to me, as no one would be walking in the fields, I realized that in the Ghetto, they had nothing but a roof over their heads—literally. Their open-sided building was their only shelter.

In the middle of May, when more and more people began working in the fields, the haystack became unsafe. One evening, Jan put me in a wheelbarrow and took me into the barn, which was connected to the house. Two horses, two cows, and Jan lived in the barn. Jan and Misha dug a hole under Jan's bed and covered it with wooden planks. On top, they put back the earth and sprinkled it with hay, leaving just a small opening so I could slide in and out. Then they covered the opening with slats and hay. And there I lived. Twice a day, while they fed and cleaned the animals, I was fed too. They let me watch while they worked with the animals. I looked forward to those times with eagerness. I thought that taking out manure from the barn was the best work one could ask for and I would have given my right arm for the privilege. One night I awoke; I was choking and could not breathe. I woke up Jan and he ran for Misha. Together, they dragged me out into the open. A few whiffs of the delicious country air and I was revived.

I think what happened was that since they had no plumbing or sewers and the barn floor was earthen, all the residue from the animals seeped through into the ground. Living in that hole I was breathing in that heavy acid smell of urine and it made me ill.

I was frightened at first, but I was overcome by the beauty of the evening. The stars shone brightly; one could almost touch them. There was a full moon and the scent of lilacs was in the air. I did not want to go back to my home underground. The night was still and no one was about, so we sat for awhile at the side of the house under a covered porch.

Off the porch was a heavy, locked door that led to a windowless storage room in which they kept their grain and smoked meat. Stairs from that room led up to the attic. That was to be my new abode. It was far better than the previous one. First, it had windows on all sides and I could rush from one to the other—carefully, of course, so as not to be seen from the outside—and look out into the world. I could then follow any activity in and around the house. In the mornings, I would read and re-read my books, including the New Testament they gave me. In the afternoon, when it got hot, I would go to the storage room and, by lamplight, embroider Maria's trousseau and sew dresses for her. I slept on the attic floor with mice scurrying around me. Whenever they had time, members of the family would come to visit with me. They were very good to me, but never missed an opportunity to remind me that I had been forsaken by my God.

Sundays were the worst. In the morning, when the church bells rang, the whole village would go to church. I would watch the happy, carefree faces, as the mothers led their children along.

In the afternoon, the merriment began; it lasted well into the night. The young people worked hard during the week in the fields, but they played even harder on Sunday. The girls in their finery would march up and down the street, while the boys would stand on the side, smoking and drinking. I could hear a happy interchange of laughter and words, After supper, a group of boys and girls would sing and dance together. Late at night, they would pair off and disappear in all directions—and I was locked in that attic.

I was eighteen that summer of '44. Some days, I'd quarrel with God and ask, "Is this what You have chosen for us?" And then I'd vow that my first trip out of that attic would be to the parish priest. I did not want to be one of "The Chosen" anymore. Then, there were other days when I saw from my window the wheat gently swaying in the fields, the flowers blooming all around, the birds frolicking, a mother hen leading her newly hatched chickens and, at the first sight of danger, sitting down and covering them with her feathers; all the other domesticated animals were playing their own games and I'd feel more at peace with God, myself, and the world. I would understand why anyone would make a pact, even with the devil, just to stay alive. I would tell God, with whom I was now on personal terms, that I wanted to live so badly, I didn't care if I had to spend the rest of my life in the attic.

No matter how bad things are, they can always be worse. And so they became as the battlefront came closer and closer. I knew that this was happening because, occasionally, I read a newspaper. Though the papers were full of lies, one could read between the lines. I could tell that those German victories were getting closer to home.

In September, a battalion of German soldiers arrived. They dispersed throughout our village. Since the Cuprinkas' house was the best-built house in the village, they promptly set up headquarters in the rooms below me. It was the first time I was close enough to look into my enemy's face. We all panicked, of course, at first. My movements and activities had to be restricted. But I was used to solitude by then. I would watch the soldiers come in and out. One hot Sunday morning, while everyone was in church, I sat on the stairs and heard the approach of heavy footsteps. They stopped at the door and, in German (which I understood), one told the other that they had an hour before the farmers returned from church to raid the storage room. I thought that this was the end. I ran up to the attic and hid in a smokeroom that was half the size of a telephone booth. An unbearable fright came over me. I said my prayers, adding, "God, I don't care anymore. Do with me as you will." With that, my fears lifted and disappeared. That morning I discovered that the good times take care of themselves, but when in trouble, one needs the belief in a Superior Being.

The soldiers set out to raid the storage room, but the door resisted all their attempts to open it! I was safe.

November came and, with it, a steady flow of German fighting forces. They brought heavy artillery and dug in, in and around the village. We could hear the firing, first from a distance, and then coming steadily closer. During the morning of October 28, the Germans seemed to disappear and the Russian soldiers suddenly appeared out of nowhere. I decided to come down from the attic, but not to tell anyone that I was Jewish. Before 1938, the region I lived in, you remember, belonged to Czechoslovakia. Now I was surrounded by Slav peasants, who spoke Czech with the dialect of their region. Since I spoke Czech fluently and had a good ear for languages, I picked up their dialect. I told the people that I lived in a nearby village and had been stranded here. It turned out that the Russians must have underrated the Germans' strength and were obviously caught in a trap. They were trying desperately to withdraw. They abandoned their machinery, which was trapped in the mud and, on foot and on stolen horses, fled towards the river. By nightfall, every haystack that had been placed in the field to make room for the harvest was burning. It was a spectacular sight. The whole village looked like a giant barn fire!

Amidst a hail of bullets, we busily carried water from the well to save the wooden structure next to the burning haystack. I must admit I was not much help. Each time a bullet whizzed by me, I would drop to the floor and spill the water. Somehow, saving a building did not seem that important to me. I would rather have saved the two injured Russian soldiers who were lying there, begging the peasants to save them (and later cursing them), but I did not dare. With their curses ringing in my ear, I approached the well. Suddenly, I was standing face to face with three German soldiers with their guns drawn, asking me in German if there were any Russian soldiers around. I shrugged my shoulders as if I did not understand.

And so, the Germans took back our part of the village, the Russians having retreated across the river. With about twenty-five other villagers whose houses were not as well built as ours, I retreated to the cellar, which was half-filled with newly harvested potatoes. We stayed there for four weeks; the fighting was fierce and constant around us. This was to be the Germans' last stand before giving up the whole region. They placed one of their low-range cannons in the front yard and the cannon fire was continuous. At night, we could hear the repeated machine gun fire coming from the river. We would sit around in circles and, a few times daily, recite the Rosary. Everyone took turns at a verse, including me. When the danger seemed to get closer, we prayed silently. I said my prayer quickly and added a Hail Mary. I felt I needed all the protection I could get. After all, I was in triple jeopardy: from the cannons, from the unsuspecting people around me, and from the Germans.

On November 25, the Germans told the villagers that they must abandon their homes. I knew that coming out of the cellar would be my end, so I convinced the Cuprinkas that to go would be a folly since all the Germans wanted was to plunder the village. Mrs. Cuprinka persuaded the Germans to let her stay behind and cook for them. Then the men dug a bunker in which Mr. Cuprinka, Misha, Maria, and I sat for the next three harrowing days and nights. As I predicted, the Germans slaughtered all the animals in the village and took everything with them. They left our livestock and grain intact because Mrs. Cuprinka was helping them. After three days of fierce fighting, the Russians crossed the river high above us and began coming over the fields, their tanks and guns blazing. Then suddenly, it was quiet. And I was free! Since this used to be Czech soil and the free Czech Army had been fighting side by side with the Russians, they treated us not as conquerors would, but like liberators. When I approached the Russian commander who had taken over the house, I told him I was Jewish and asked him if he knew what had happened to my family. He pointed to the stove and said bluntly that they went up in smoke. Seeing my disbelief, he promised that as soon as the roads were safe, he would let me ride into town on one of his trucks and see for myself.

Chapter 6

Finally Free

As in a dream—or, rather, a nightmare—I got off his truck. I walked straight home along the familiar streets.. I rang the bell and a woman answered. I asked her if the Reisman family—my family—lived there. She said "No" and slammed the door in my face. I stood there in a daze, not knowing where to turn. I was weak, my knees were buckling under me, and it was getting late. I could not return to the village. I knew one thing: I did not want to meet any of our Gentile neighbors. I spotted the son-in-law of Ari Friedman, one of our Jewish neighbors. I called to him. When I told him who I was, he could not believe his eyes. He said I was the first of three Jewish girls, and the first of ten people from our town, who had found safety in hiding.

I told him my story and added that I didn't have a place to stay. He took me to a store that he and his partners ran. One of his partners was named "Harry." It was a custom tailoring shop, belonging to their former Jewish boss, who had not come back. In the four weeks during which the town was being liberated, they had done a flourishing business sewing uniforms for the Russian officers. There were a few rooms in the back of the store and the men slept on mattresses they had taken from Jewish homes. One of the rooms had a couch, which they gave to me.

Also staying with them was a Hungarian commander. I learned that he had been instrumental in helping them escape en route to a concentration camp. It had been October, 1944 and this commander had orders to deliver his Jews to the nearest concentration camp. The Russians were close on their tails because Europe was now in the process of being liberated city by city. Everyone knew the Germans had lost the war. But the commander had two choices: he could follow his orders and eventually end up as a prisoner-of-war or he could confide in his men and tell them the truth. He chose the latter and they changed their route, heading for our home ground, where the

men knew both the terrain and the language. There they hid in a
barn. The commander changed his clothes, put on the yellow
band of the Jews and, together with his men, he was liberated
by the Russians. About two hundred men escaped the death
camps this way. Out of gratitude to the commander, Grandpa
and his partner kept him with them.

Most of the Jewish homes were occupied by Gentiles, and
they showed no signs of giving these homes back to the returning people. Some homes were only looted, and groups of men
moved into these. In one such home, one of Grandpa's friends, a
gay fellow and a good cook, set up housekeeping and we all
went there for our meals.

The boys gave the commander and me jobs in the store. We
tried to do whatever we could to earn our keep. That shop became the center of Jewish activities. At one time or another,
every Jew would stop in and visit. Jews were on the go. A sur-
vivor of the Warsaw Ghetto was on his way to Israel, undaunted
by the fact that the war was still raging around us. People were
coming from or going to Rumania, Poland, and the liberated
parts of Hungary. We would huddle together, telling each other
the tales of our survival (one more incredible than the other);
singing Jewish songs; and ignoring the non-Jewish world
around us. The boys would take me out for walks or ice cream.
Grandpa encouraged me to go, saying that the work would wait
for me. Grandpa got me clothing from a Russian soldier, so that
I could get out of my peasant clothes. He sent me to a beauty
parlor. When I refused to take his money, he told me that he
would take it out of my salary. But I never got my salary because, by the end of the month, I was engaged to the boss. I have
been working for him ever since.

We were to marry that January of 1945. All the planning,
shopping, and preparations fell on me. Since our two bridges
had been blown up and the hastily built new one was too far
away, I had to carry baskets full of meat on my arm across the
frozen river.

A day before the wedding, I witnessed a fascinating discussion among three men. They were debating several questions.
The first question was, Could the *schochet*, who was available,
perform our marriage ceremony? "Well," said one of them,
"since there is no Rabbi, he could." Then another question was
posed: Would it be a kosher wedding if the bride didn't go to

the *Mikva*? The first man said, "It depends on who the bride is." "In this case," answered the other, "it couldn't be a kosher wedding, as I was the daughter of a pious, observant, scholarly Jew." "But," replied the third, "in view of the fact that the *Mikva* has not been used for nine months, and we have not the authority to make it usable, the marriage will be kosher without the bride going to the *Mikva*."

These were men who had spent up to four years in Russia under the most inhuman working conditions. They were beaten and shot at by the German, Hungarian, and Russian soldiers. They had practically no medical help and no medicines. Grandpa had typhus and worked throughout with high fever, because to tell someone that you were sick was tantamount to death. In Davidka, there was a small hospital filled with Jewish patients, most suffering from typhus. Rather than waste their drugs on Jews, the Germans set the hospital ablaze and surrounded it with machine gun fire.

The men's stay on the battlefront culminated with a march in -40° weather, sometimes without shoes. They couldn't sit down, because if they did, they would freeze. They marched for four months without any food rations. They lived off whatever the frozen fields would yield. Grandpa once lived for weeks on a frozen piece of butter! They would cut meat from the frozen carcasses of horses that lined the roads and carry it for days before they got a chance to cook it. Once, Grandpa and a friend of his ate some horse meat, and the next day his friend died of food poisoning. They slept in whatever shelter they could find; sometimes there were so many of them together that there wasn't enough room for everyone to sit down in.

Your Grandpa tells an awesome story about that period of time: It was January, 1943. Grandpa was marching with the combined German and Hungarian armies toward Moscow. The Russians were determined to stop the advancing enemy at all costs, so they fought fiercely with everything they had. Grandpa's regiment arrived just as the Russians broke through enemy lines. The carnage and mayhem were tremendous. The German/Hungarian army, broken both morally and militarily, began to retreat, relentlessly pursued by the Russians. Their motorized vehicles, unaccustomed to the harsh soil of the Russian winter, broke down, so they were forced to march on foot.

After three months of marching, the Hungarians stopped to

regroup and consolidate their forces. Four hundred men—tailors, shoemakers, and mechanics—were selected to be shipped to Kiev, the home of the new Hungarian headquarters and warehouses. Your Grandpa was one of the four hundred. The train they rode was an open freight flat-deck, very cold and uncomfortable, so Grandpa and three of his friends hid in the warm, enclosed caboose. The train chugged along slowly and the exhausted men slept. Suddenly the motion ceased. Grandpa awoke to find that the caboose was no longer attached to its train. It stood alone in a railroad yard in some God-forsaken village in the Ukraine. It seems that while they had slept, the caboose got uncoupled from the train.

Fearfully, Grandpa and his friends approached the railroad station and were promptly arrested. They were led into the German commandant's office. They explained their situation to no avail. They were branded partisans, tried then and there, with the Ukranian militia given orders to take them out to the woods to be shot. On the way out, one of the militiamen took Grandpa's watch—one of the two sole possessions he had at the time. The other was his father's *tefilin*. As they walked out of the railway station, Grandpa noticed two Hungarian officers. As he passed them, he shouted in Hungarian, "This man has my watch. Help me and it will be yours." Watches were a most prized possession at that time.

The Hungarian officers stopped the militiamen, demanding, "Where are you taking our men?" As it turned out, these Hungarian officers were also heading for the Hungarian headquarters in Kiev and, by a twist of fate, had missed the train. They assured the commandant that they would take full responsibility for these men. Then they retrieved Grandpa's watch and, together, Grandpa, his friends, and the officers hopped the next train to Kiev. And so these officers snatched Grandpa and his friends from the hands of their would-be executioners. They also gave them a loaf of bread, the first they had eaten in months!

Grandpa was saved by a wristwatch and lived to tell us his tale. But thousands less fortunate were left lying in the woods—or, by the roadside all across Russia, some were buried in shallow graves, others not buried at all. Out of sixty thousand men, only five thousand returned.

And when they did arrive home, what did they find? Their

homes and businesses had been plundered; the life savings of generations were down the drain. Mothers, fathers, sisters, brothers, wives, and children were lost. Why? Because they were born Jews.

You would think that these men would be so bitter that they would denounce the Jewish religion, with all of its traditions. Instead they sat splitting hairs over how to interpret the ancient laws of that religion! It's true that our Bible and Talmud have kept us alive for these 2,000 years!

Our wedding took place on January 7, 1945 in the home of a woman who was a known Jewish sympathizer and who, by that time, ran a restaurant in her home for the returning Jewish men. All the Jewish traditions were observed. They erected a makeshift *chupah* and the *ksuba* was handwritten. The only two Jewish women in town led me under the *chupah*. One of the women and her husband were the only Jewish couple in town. They baked the challah, because there were no Jewish bakers. No invitations were sent out, but every Jew in town was there, including the Russian Jewish soldiers stationed in and out of town. It was a happy wedding. The Gypsies played; there was enough vodka, wine, and food for everyone. We did not look like the remains of a beaten people. If there were any tears shed that day by anyone, they were shed in private.

When I think back to our wedding, it seemed to me it was more of an affirmation, a celebration of life, than what you would imagine a wedding to be. Here we were, two people barely out of the clutches of extermination, surrounded by hundreds of Jews—some old friends, some new ones, others we had never met, each of them back from the edge of an abyss. Men and women proclaiming to the world that had tried to destroy them (and almost succeeded) that they would not be defeated. Those of us who survived meant to go on living!

My trousseau consisted of one nightgown that Grandpa managed to buy on the black market. The wedding gown had been borrowed from a Gentile friend. I had thought of every detail, except one. Where would we spend our wedding night? As I told you before, Grandpa and his partner slept on mattresses on the floor in a room behind their shop. I had been sleeping in another room on the couch. Some time during the reception, Grandpa suddenly realized that no provisions had been made. The situation was quickly remedied, however. A Russian soldier lady who was dancing with his partner offered to share her apartment with him.

And so Grandma and Grandpa were married and lived happily ever after. True—but the road to happy ever after was not an easy one. Sometimes it was fraught with peril, sometimes amusing. Often it was most unusual, starting with our honeymoon. I would like to tell you about that, and the journey that took us through six countries of Europe, culminating in America.

As we were walking home with a neighbor after the wedding we realized, to our dismay, that Ari had taken the only key to

At our wedding—January 7, 1945.

the shop with him. The shop was in an arcade. Instead of going through the arcade to the shop's main entrance, we walked through the courtyard to try the back window. There was a bar on the window, which Grandpa and the neighbor tore out with their bare hands. Then they broke the window, climbed in, and opened the door to my "bridal suite." To our horror, we discovered that the shop had been broken into and looted. The racket we raised trying to get in had scared the thieves away. The arcade was strewn with parts of uniforms that they had dropped as they made their getaway.

I must explain to you the enormity of the situation. The uniforms that Grandpa had been making were for the highest-ranking officers. They had provided their own fabrics, and goodness knows how they had gotten them; fabric was so hard to come by. There were no stores. A Russian officer could have had gold to pay with, but he still could not buy a new dress uniform. Among the uniforms that were stolen some were finished, some unfinished; most were irreplaceable. While I sat on the mattress in my brand new nightgown, Grandpa sat in the police station fighting for his life, his fate hanging by a thread. Luckily for us, they caught the thieves. A Jewish soldier in the military police came to Grandpa's rescue and he was released. We dared not spend another night at the shop, but where were we to go?

Most of the Jewish homes were occupied by Gentiles who would not move out. Some houses had been looted and were uninhabitable. And the Russians showed no interest in providing housing for the returning Jews. But the same soldiers who had helped Grandpa at the police station helped us again. One home, previously belonging to a very rich Jew, was occupied by a few Polish women of questionable character. They had come there with the German army and were left behind. They were on the list to be deported back to Poland in a few days. The soldiers saw to it that the apartment was vacated that very day and that I had my "honeymoon suite." Ah, the spoils of war! Riches beyond our dreams. A completely furnished, huge apartment, complete with fine bone china, porcelain figurines, linens, and antique furniture—and a bathroom. Even the ghosts of the former occupants remained to haunt us.

Within two weeks, another Jewish couple got married and they and the bride's brother came to share our home. The apartment had a magnificent large salon, where we would hold "open house." All the new returnees would come by and we would party. Someone would bring a Gypsy with him who would play for us, and we would dance and laugh and tell stories of our individual survivals. We cried and sang Jewish songs and strengthened one another.

Then I became pregnant. Whoever said, "What you don't know can't hurt you" was right in our case. We knew nothing of family planning or that it was necessary to prepare a nursery for the new baby. We were ecstatic and so was everyone else. This would be the first Jewish child to be born out of the ruins.

The war was raging around us, but we knew the outcome was inevitable. With imminent victory for the Russians came rumors that they were planning to annex our hometown and that we would forever belong to Russia. In a few months, this actually happened.

Our Russian Jewish soldier friends urged us to leave. Since I was expecting a baby, we decided not to take chances. Instead of waiting for the war to end, we left immediately. Grandpa took his *tefilin*, which he had carried with him all through Russia. I took a miniature porcelain table (one of my wedding gifts), some Hebrew books from my father's vast collection, my brother's Kiddish cup (which I had found at our house in the attic), a minimum of personal clothing, and packed them in that suitcase my mother had sent after me when I was staying at the Cuprinkas.

But where should we go? The war was still raging around us. In the rest of Hungary and Czechoslovakia the Germans were fiercely resisting the advancing Russian army. The only fully liberated country was Rumania, so that was where we headed. We took the train from Uzhorod and, after traveling through Transylvania, we landed in Oradea-Mare, Rumania.

We rented a furnished room. On our second day there I awoke to see Grandpa dressed. "Are you going out already?" I inquired. "No," he replied, "I came back for lunch. I found a job." We had not known a soul in Rumania. He had walked from one tailor shop to the next till he had found a job. This was your Grandpa. Unlike Shakespeare's Hamlet, Grandpa never stopped to ponder "To be or not to be." After all he went through, not once did he stop to wallow in self-pity, even for a minute. While lesser men stopped to lick their wounds, he

fashioned his own world from all this madness. He had a family
to support!

The worst was finally over; the war ended and with this came
new hope. Spring was in the air. There was an abundance of
flowers; the markets were brimming with fruits and other edible
goodies. And we were young and happy. We spent two idyllic
months in Rumania.

Our room overlooked a small river. We joined the natives to
fish. We fried what we caught over an open fire. We stayed out
till late at night, climbing in our apartment window so as not to
waken our old landlady. Often, we ate our meals in a small restaurant, where we met other survivors.

Then, one morning in early July, there was a knock at the
door, and there stood Grandpa's brother, Joe. I couldn't imagine
how he had found us. As in a jungle (and the early days of post-
war Europe were a jungle), there was no mail, no form of communication except homing pigeons and tom-tom drums. But the
tom-tom drums were beating. The returnees from the concentration camps and forced labor camps were the homing pigeons.
They crisscrossed Europe by foot and train and, wherever they
stopped, they would spread the news: I met a man who met a
man who told me your brother or mother is alive or dead.

After his liberation from a concentration camp, Joe had
headed straight for Debrecen (Hungary), where his fiance lived.
She, too, had just returned from a concentration camp, along
with her sister and mother. It was there that Joe learned of our
whereabouts and came to fetch us.

The Rumanian town we lived in was only an overnight ride
from Debrecen, but there was no public transportation whatsoever. Joe and Grandpa found a Russian soldier who was willing to take us and other unsuspecting passengers across the
border. We traveled in a dilapidated army truck that had no
seats. We sat on wooden planks. The driver, a Russian soldier
with a bad hangover, stopped at every twist and turn in the
road to throw up. I wanted to join him, only I was too scared to
open my eyes—or my mouth. We rode for hours at breakneck
speed, first up and then down the high mountain range that
separated Rumania from Hungary. The high serpentine road,
the overhanging cliffs, and the deep gorges below us only
added to our panic. But we made it.

After a short stay in Debrecen, Grandpa and Joe decided to

try their hand at black-marketing—the only way to go, according to Joe. So, armed with a few pounds of Hungarian paprika, we began our trek towards the West. Our first stop was Budapest.

We headed straight for my cousin, Tilus. After glancing at my protruding belly, she announced that we were stark raving mad for having a baby at this time and for coming to war-torn Budapest, which was under Russian siege and devastated. When she heard of Joe's grandiose plans to take the paprika to Prague and bring some exchange goods back, she put her foot down. She told Grandpa to go without me, find a home or a semblance of one, and then come back for me.

Joe and Grandpa left the same day, for there was no place for them to sleep. I was invited to share Tilus's bed. As soon as I turned out the lights, an army of bed bugs attacked me. They sapped my blood. If I killed one, a hundred others would come to avenge its demise. I spent those next two weeks sleeping in a chair near a window, and with my fellow "homing pigeons" ate many a meal in soup kitchens and out of tin cans.

Grandpa came back a conquering hero. He had not only sold the paprika, but had brought fabrics back with him, which he sold for a small fortune. Best of all, he had found an apartment. Well, not really an apartment, but a promise of one in Teplice-Sanov, Sudeten, which was part of Czechoslovakia.

Here I must pause again to give you a little history lesson. The town I grew up in and the whole region that had been given to Hungary in 1938 had now been annexed to Russia. The one concession made to the Czechs was that anyone who wanted to could leave this new section of Russia to live in what was still Czechoslovakia. Of course, most of the Jews, who came back and found their families gone, their houses and businesses plundered, and the government unsympathetic to their plight, opted to do just that. And they found a haven in the Sudeten. This area had previously been the home of people of German descent who had invited and embraced Hitler when he entered Czechoslovakia. These people prospered under the Germans, but that prosperity was coming to an end. The Czechs were now rounding up all these self-declared Germans and unceremoniously shipping them to their "fatherland." Their fully furnished apartments, as well as their businesses, were being given to the returning Jews and those Jews who opted to leave

Russian occupation. Here the wheels of justice were turning because those apartments and businesses had probably originally belonged to the Czech Jews anyway. Officially, they called this action "repatriation." In other words, you were a German patriot, so now go live in Germany.

Grandpa found a buddy of his who was serving in the free Czech army and already had one of these apartments. He asked Grandpa to bring me to Sudeten with the understanding that we could stay with him initially. He promised to use his influence to obtain an apartment of our own for us. Of course, I was overjoyed, full of anticipation. I wanted to start out right away, but Grandpa was exhausted from the trip and wanted to rest for two or three days. But where? There was no room at my cousin's; they already shared their small apartment with another relative. Jewish agencies provided shelters for refugees, but they offered mostly cots in dorms that separated the sexes, since most refugees were single. Finally, towards evening, we somehow found a small hotel. We had very modest expectations—a good night's sleep and a little privacy. As we walked in, a man in an enclosed window in a booth asked Grandpa how long he wanted the room for—one hour or two. When Grandpa told him he wanted it for the whole night, he threw an appreciative glance at me and said to Grandpa, "Well, it's your money!" He then quoted us an astronomical price, but we paid it. We walked into the lobby with our room key, but the hostess said our room was not ready and we would have to wait. After a while, Grandpa became impatient and asked how long it would take to get the room ready. "Well," the woman said, as she looked me over, her eyes stopping at my protruding belly, "the room is still occupied." Then she called into the room, "Hurry up there, this is not one of your tarts. This is a virtuous woman." She must have reasoned that anyone crazy enough to become pregnant during the war must be naive, and therefore virtuous.

A few agonizing minutes passed while I wished the ground would swallow me and save me from this embarrassment. The woman took great pains to insure that our stay there was pleasant. The room had been cleaned, the bed linen immaculately laundered, and the bedbugs did not bite (although I have a sneaking suspicion that the bad reputation of the hotel kept them away). Some things, however, were beyond the woman's control, for instance, the knock on our door in the middle of the night. It was the police and Grandpa was ordered out of the room. While he was interrogated outside, I was interrogated inside. They wanted to make sure that our stories matched. We had a hard time convincing the police that we were really married. Luckily for me, we had proof, so I was not carted away with the other ladies of the evening. While I was not present when they raided Minsky's, I sure as hell remember how it felt when they raided that bordello in Budapest. We left the next day in a hurry.

It seemed that all of Europe was on the move. The survivors of the concentration camps, soldiers of all nationalities, prisoners of war—all were heading in different directions, relying on the railroads to take them home. Most trains were overloaded and, at best, unpredictable. Bratislava had a major railroad station, where most of the trains going to and from Germany, Czechoslovakia, Hungary, and Rumania converged.

We arrived there the next day, hoping to catch a train to Prague. Tickets were not necessary; timetables were not available. You got to the railroad station—you and thousands of others—and waited for a train to come, hoping it was going to your destination. But there was no need to worry. If you did not catch a train today, one might come tomorrow or the next day, or the next. An enormously large and restless crowd stood waiting for the next train, which, rumor had it, would arrive shortly, heading for Prague. One quick glance at that crowd and it was evident that all who wished to go to Prague would not make it on the next train. So Grandpa bribed one of the trainmen, who took him out to the railroad yard, and there he boarded the train. At long last, the train approached the railroad station, its whistle blowing triumphantly. Out of the window of a first-class compartment Grandpa was waving frantically. All I had to do was to board the train and I had a reserved seat. Simple, right? But the whistle of the train brought out the beast in that teeming gathering of humanity and the group of people turned into a charging herd of elephants. They pushed and shoved and, I pulled back instinctively, trying to protect my protruding belly. (It was early August and I was either in my late sixth or seventh month. I was not sure; I hadn't seen a doctor in months.)

Just as in the old Indian movies, in a few minutes all that humanity was in the train, on top of the train, on the steps of the train, some hanging on with just one hand. Inside the train people were packed in like sardines. There was no room, except for the seat Grandpa was holding for me, but no one was willing to get off to let me on. So there I was, standing alone on the platform, with Grandpa hollering at me from the window. A serious situation calling for drastic measures. A couple of guys jumped off the stairs and, together with the conductor, while the crowd shouted multilingual encouragement, hoisted me up and pushed me and my belly through the window. Then they all burst into wild applause. The conductor blew his whistle and we were off to our new home.

Under normal circumstances, the ride from Bratislava to Prague takes a few hours. Our train, overweight and bulging with teeming humanity, chugged along at a snail's pace. At every approaching overhang, they had to warn those on top to duck, lest they be decapitated (which, by the way, did happen on another train). The next day, we arrived in Prague. Just a few more hours on a train and we would be at our destination—Teplice–Sanov.

Just outside the railroad station we headed for a shelter, where we would spend the night. We came upon a crowd watching a procession of hundreds of people, mostly men marching by, or rather being led away. They were all German—old men and young boys—wearing the required white band that identified them as Germans.

The crowd was comprised mainly of men and some women, who had just come back from concentration or forced labor camps. They all jeered and hurled epithets at the Germans. Every once in a while, a figure would dart out of the crowd and hit the passersby. Others would join in, but then someone would restrain them, saying, "Brothers, we are above that. They are in the hands of the law." Most of us were crying. Again, instinctively protecting the tiny life inside of me, I pulled back. I studied the crowd. The hate that was in their eyes was frightening; I knew where it came from. These people were the survivors of Buchenwald, Auschwitz, and Treblinka, where they had witnessed firsthand the cruelest atrocities that modern man had inflicted on other human beings. They had been in cattle cars; they watched loved ones being shot at, starved to death, beaten, and tortured. They worked the ovens where they were exterminated. They buried the dead in mass graves. They smelled the stench of the burning flesh. And, all the time, the

German soldiers stood in front of their eyes, intimidating, bullying, and threatening.

I, on the other hand, by a quirk of fate, was spared all that. Where they met cruelty and degradation, I met kindness and caring. While I underwent my own kind of hell, loneliness, and numbing fear, I did not meet my enemy face to face. I saw no torture. I did not see my mother beaten, as did others.

I realized then that this would set me forever apart from them. I would forever feel guilty for not being there. Perhaps by not being there, I could not participate fully in their rage. At the same time, we fully share the destruction of our families, the deep and indescribable loss that time does not heal.

When I looked at those survivors, knowing what they had gone through, I marveled at their restraint. At the same time, for the sake of, or maybe because of, that tiny life in me, I could feel some pity for those young boys (really children) in that procession and give them the benefit of the doubt as to their guilt or innocence.

How naive we were, though, about "the hands of the law." We were convinced that the world would be outraged at the fate of those who perished and thus sympathetic to the plight of the survivors. We had no doubt that this outrage would lead the world to search out the S.S., the Nazis, the keepers of the concentration camps, and punish them. We thought, for sure, that the survivors of the camps would be helped to rebuild their lives, to reclaim their homes and, if that was not possible, to relocate them far from the land soaked with the blood of their loved ones.

Nothing could have been further from the truth. Except for the few very high-ranking officials who were charged at the Nuremberg trials, the guilty were permitted to scatter and fade into the woodwork. While victims of their persecution were languishing in D.P. camps in Germany or wandering around the globe, as we were; while the American Consulates were laying obstacles in the paths of the survivors, keeping them from immigrating to the U.S. with stringent quotas, many known Nazis and S.S. were, with the help of the C.I.A. and other organizations, whisked into the U.S. and various South American countries to start new lives under new identities. So much for world "justice."

Chapter 7

Grandpa's Family

While this book is really my story, it would be incomplete if I didn't tell you about how Grandpa's family emerged from those terrible times. Their lives were also turned upside down.

Grandpa's mother was only thirty-seven years old when she died, leaving behind six children: Roslyn, age one and a half; Grandpa, age four; Mendle, five; Miriam, eight; Leibish, eleven; and Sol, sixteen. Grandpa's only memory of his mother is of the day they went to the photographer to take a family picture when he was four. He remembers holding her hand while walking to the photographer. At the end of that same year she died during childbirth. Grandpa's only other memory of his mother is when he sat beside the hearse that carried her and the stillborn twins she had given birth to.

Their father was devastated. The loss of a wife and mother is always a traumatic experience, but the tragedy is compounded when it happens in childbirth, when the whole family is expecting a happy event and instead ends up bereaved and distraught. And there were no uncles, aunts or grandparents to console and nurture them.

The family itself had only recently been transplanted from Poland. They had come to Uzhorod only two-and-one-half years before, having fled the advancing Russian army and the marauding Cossacks. The other members of their father's family—three brothers and a sister—had fled to America at the same time. Their father had refused to join them. A Chasidic Jew, deeply religious, he would not bring his children to the "Heathen Land." A good businessman with connections in the fur trade, he quickly established himself in this new town and prospered. He bought a house and hired a maid to help out when business kept him away from home. His business sometimes demanded that he travel and stay away for days at a time. Although the maid kept things under control at home, there was

This photo, taken in 1917, shows my husband, Harry standing at his mother's right. Others (from left to right) are: Miriam, Roslyn, Mendel, Sol and Leibish.

no one of stature and authority to care for his grieving children. He really needed to remarry.

And so it was that, soon after, he returned from one of his trips to Poland not only with furs, but with a new wife. Grandpa remembers her fondly. She was basically fair, hardworking, and took care of the children. Everyone took to her immediately, except Roslyn, who was just too young when her mother had died to accept a replacement. She was a sensitive child whose mother had just disappeared and she could not comprehend why. She craved attention but the adults around her were too busy. Her father was often away on business and her new mother was overwhelmed by the large family she had inherited.

During the next ten years, Grandpa's stepmother gave birth to seven children—Joe, Icu, Benyu, Paul, Dave, Toby and Moishe; Sol, in order to evade the draft, came to America; Leibish left home, never to be heard from again; Mendel died of consumption; and Miriam emigrated to Israel.

Then tragedy struck. Grandpa's father became ill and was diagnosed as having cancer, a rare diagnosis in those days. Our town did not have the medical facilities to deal with his illness, so he traveled to Germany for treatment. Later, he went back to have his leg amputated. After long, protracted periods of recuperation, several setbacks and many more trips to Germany for treatment, he died.

His death left his large family destitute. He had been a deeply religious man, who believed in God and his fellow men. While he was earning large amounts of money, instead of protecting his family's future, he helped out everyone who needed it by lending them money. He trusted his fellow men, but they let him down. All his family was left with were uncollectible I.O.U.s.

Despite the fact that there was a depression in America, Sol fulfilled his father's dying wish and brought Roslyn to America in 1938. Grandpa had accompanied her to Prague, where she boarded the last ship to leave Czechoslovakia before war engulfed it.

Back at home, Grandpa had become the breadwinner, but in the spring of 1940 he was drafted into the reserves and sent to a labor camp about 60 kilometers from home. In the winter he was allowed to return home. In the spring of 1941 Grandpa was again sent to this labor camp and his brother, Joe, who was twenty-one years old, was sent to a labor camp in Yugoslavia. As before, Grandpa was allowed to go home in the winter. In the spring of 1942 he was sent to the labor camp again, except this time, after about two months, he was shipped out to Russia, leaving at home his mother, his brother Icu, who was 19; Benyu, 17; Paul, 16; Dave, 13; Toby, 10 (the only girl); and Moishe, 8. These are the recollections of Paul who, together with his family, was taken to the same ghetto my family was in.

Grandpa's family had lived on the outskirts of town and, Paul tells me, that is where the collection of Jews began in March, 1944. Stunned, bewildered, and numb with fear, they were marched through town, carrying whatever possessions they were allowed—clothing, bedding, and food. They took whatever they could carry. Because they were among the first arrivals in the ghetto, they were also among the lucky ones. They were assigned a corner of a room in a great big storage house, sheltered from the cold and the rain. The food they managed to bring with them, together with their rations, given, kept them from starving.

Once the initial bewilderment and shock wore off, they were reassured by rumors that they would be taken to work camps. They were all young, strong, and hopeful.

One day, about five weeks later, without any prior notice or explanation, they were ordered to leave the ghetto and board buses. The buses took them to the railroad station and there, under the watchful eyes of the Czendors, they were herded into cattle cars. They were packed in so tightly that there was only enough room to sit down in with their knees hunched up. The cattle cars were dark and windowless, with just a slight opening at the top for air. With great finality, the doors were locked and bolted from the outside. With the bolt of the lock, the shouting and crying, the pushing and shoving, the great pandemonium suddenly stopped. A palpable hush fell over the crowd as the enormity of their desperate situation sunk in. The boys huddled around their mother as if to protect her. Of course, they had no inkling of the unspeakable horror that was awaiting them; they were still optimistic about their destination and reassured their mother that the four boys would work as hard as necessary to provide for and protect her.

They rode for three days and nights. With each passing hour, their optimism waned. The speeding train rushed through the night, taking them further and further away from home. With each clang of the train's wheels, their fear of the unknown got stronger and stronger. That fear became so overpowering and paralyzing that it mercifully blocked Paul's thoughts. He does not remember eating anything or relieving himself. He does not remember anyone else doing so either. He only remembers that the train would stop periodically at a station, the door would open, and a few people from each car would be permitted to go down and get fresh water.

As the train sped past small-town depots, the passengers would crane their necks to see if they could make out the names of the towns, trying to figure out where they were heading. But this was to no avail; no markers were visible.

Finally, the train stopped and, within seconds, the doors of the cattle cars opened and they were in Auschwitz. Urgent shouts of "*Heraus!*" (get out) were hurled at them. They were ordered to leave everything behind and immediately form a line outside the cattle cars, where they were confronted by German soldiers and snarling dogs. It all happened so quickly. Each person was told by soldiers to walk to one of two lines. The able-bodied were herded down one line, the older people and children, down another. Young mothers carrying their babies were automatically put into the line with the elderly. Most mothers held their children's hands; if they resisted letting their children go to their assigned line alone, they were pushed into the line with them. Needless to say, most mothers resisted—

Paul's mother among them. She went to her death (for that line lead straight to the gas chambers) holding onto her two youngest, twelve-year-old Toby and ten-year old Moishe. Dave was lucky. Though only fifteen, he was tall for his age and, flanked by his three older brothers—Icu, Benyu, and Paul—he found himself on the other line. He was one of the youngest survivors from our hometown, as a matter of fact. Only three other boys of the same age returned from the concentration camp.

The four brothers were herded into the camp, where, in the ensuing melée, they got separated. Paul and Dave ended up not far away, in a camp that supplied workers for a coal mine; they stayed there until January, 1945.

Dave was assigned to the children's barracks and he and other young boys did odd chores.

The coal pits were opened and mined twenty-four hours a day. Paul was assigned to the night shift. They lined up at 8:30 at night and then walked for half an hour to work. They descended 450 feet underground, worked an 8-hour shift, and then walked back to camp in the morning. Every Jew was assigned to a Polish miner. Guards were constantly watching to make sure that each load was full; otherwise there was hell to pay. The work was very hard.

Back at camp after work, they showered, changed back into prison garb, and ate their one daily ration of food. It consisted of a thin slice of German pumpernickel bread, a thin slice of blood-wurst, and watery soup. They went to bed hungry, woke up hungry, and went to work hungry.

When the men complained about the work's being too hard and the food rations too meager, they were told their complaints would be redressed. In the meantime, the numbers of the complainers (they all had numbers tattooed on their arms) were recorded. The next Saturday morning, everyone was ordered to line up, the complainers were stripped naked and whipped within an inch of their lives. Needless to say, no one complained after that.

Once a month, the Gestapo would come into the camp. The men would have to line up naked and the Gestapo would poke and look over each person. Those found to be too emaciated and unfit to work were taken away. The men would tremble with fear because, by then, they knew the fate awaiting them: the gas chamber. Only the young, the very strong, and the resourceful managed to survive.

Paul was all of the above. He worked very hard and the

Polish man he was assigned to liked that and befriended him. Each day, he would give Paul some extra bread and Paul, in turn, would literally give him the shirt off his back. Every morning when they went to work, they would each be issued a clean shirt (they had rooms full of clothes that had been taken from the Jews). Paul would get to pick out the best shirt they had. He would put that one on and the man would give him another shirt, which he would wrap around his shoe. When he got to the mine, he would take off the shirt he was wearing, give it to the Pole, take the other shirt off his shoe and wear that one all day. By the evening, it would be wet from perspiration and black from the coal. Straight into the laundry it went. And the process would begin again the next day—trading shirts for extra food. This way, he kept himself and Dave better fed.

In January, the Allied troops closed in and the camps had to be evacuated. The men marched on foot for about three days. It was an unusually cold winter, the roads were snowy and icy, and all the inmates had were their cotton prison garb, torn shoes, and very little else. Those who were lucky had sheets or blankets to wrap around their backs and feet.

At night they stopped in open fields. The ground was covered with snow and frozen ice and they were ordered to lay down and rest. As tired as they were, they refused. They were chilled to the bone already and that frozen ground was not inviting. Still, the soldiers emptied a volley of bullets in the air and threatened to shoot anyone left standing. Dave and Paul had one torn blanket between them, so they huddled together and warmed each other. Finally, they arrived in Buchenwald, another infamous camp.

After two weeks in Buchenwald, they found themselves on the road again, forced to escape from the advancing Allied forces. On these marches, no rations were issued. Weakened and exhausted, with little fat left on their bodies to draw energy from, they dragged on. Those who fell behind or sat down were shot on the spot. No one was left behind alive.

Paul's luck held out. When they arrived at the new camp, he was assigned to work in the laundry, where they washed and disinfected clothes. Once again he had an opportunity to barter clothes and blankets for food. One day, while he was working in that laundry, the door opened and in walked his brother Joe. Paul was so excited to see Joe that he forgot to tell him that Dave was there too. They walked together to Paul's barrack and there the unsuspecting Joe found his other brother, Dave. The three brothers embraced and cried tears of joy and sorrow.

Joe told them of his odyssey. He too, had marched on foot for weeks, finally to arrive at this camp after having suffered the hardships of the forced labor camp in Servia, Yugoslavia. The brothers took it as a good omen that providence had brought the three of them together. Together, they would strengthen and watch over each other and increase their chance of survival.

By early spring, the Allies were once again closing in and the brothers were forced to march once more. They arrived in Flasenberg, where rumors were flying that the Allies were expected to overtake the camp after midnight. But the rumors were just that. They were ordered to march once again. In the daytime, they would forage the fields and woods for beets and other edible roots. At night, they would sleep in the woods. By now, the soil was muddy from the melted snow and the spring rain. Paul hooked his feet on the low-lying branches, so he would not slip deeper down into the mud slopes. These marches proved to be the undoing of many of the people who had survived the harshness of the camps. Their bodies were weakened, their spirits and hopes were drained, and they just gave up.

On April 23, at 4 o'clock in the morning, suddenly low-flying planes swooped down over them. As they scurried and jumped to the sides of the road, a column of tanks rolled by, under the cover of more low-flying planes. The long-awaited Americans had finally arrived! As they passed the bedraggled ragtag group, they showered the people with chocolates, chewing gum, cheeses, crackers, and—joy of joys—K rations.

The German soldiers and the concentration camp guards threw away their guns, changed into civilian clothes, and joined the liberated inmates on their march. The minute the Americans arrived, the German soldiers seemed to develop collective amnesia. It was difficult to find one who remembered guarding a concentration camp or had heard of a place like Auschwitz or Buchenwald.

The war was finally over for Paul, Dave and Joe; they were free at last. But their ordeal was far from over. Their chances for survival depended on getting some nourishment. Dave was getting very weak. As they passed a farmhouse, Joe jumped out of the line and ran into the house to requisition supplies. He was successful but, by the time he emerged victorious, the others had already been swept away with the crowd. So Joe proceeded alone to Debrecen, Hungary, where he hoped his fiancée would be waiting for him.

Paul and Dave, in the meantime, continued on, realizing that there was no chance of Joe's catching up with them. By nightfall, they reached a hayloft, where they hid and rested. In the morning, Dave was racked with fever and dysentery. In desperation, Paul knocked on a farm door. The farmers fed him, but they could do nothing for Dave. They told him that there was an American headquarters ten miles away. Paul found a small cart in the hayloft and placed Dave in it. Summoning his last ounce of strength, he pushed Dave through ten miles of muddy country roads.

By the time they arrived at the American headquarters, Dave was delirious. There was no doctor or medication available, but the Americans called in a German doctor from the nearby P.O.W. camp. The doctor shook his head. "Too late," he declared. But Paul would have none of that. He created a scene: "Don't you give up on him!" he shouted. "We did not go through hell to give up now. Your army must have a doctor; I demand a real doctor." Hearing the commotion, the commander came out. He ordered an ambulance, which drove them twenty miles to a German hospital. The hospital was woefully understaffed, there were a few doctors and a skeleton staff of nurses comprised of nuns. The diagnosis was a critical case of typhus. Dave needed medication, which the army promised to supply, and constant care, which Paul supplied. As a matter of fact, Paul promised the nuns that if they helped Dave, he would help to nurse the other patients too. And so it was. Paul got a room in town and worked for weeks side-by-side with the nuns. Dave's recovery was slow and his recuperation even slower. The hospital was full of typhus patients and, in the end, Paul came down with typhus too. But by that time, there was a steady supply of medicine, the treatment had been perfected and, most important, Paul was in good physical condition. Consequently, his recovery was easier and faster.

Paul and Dave stayed at the hospital until they both fully recovered their health and strength. Only then did they start their long trek home. It was early summer by then.

They walked ambitiously, stopping in shelters for rest and food. In one of these shelters near Czechoslovakia, they found out from another homing pigeon that their brother Harry was alive, married, and living in Teplice-Sanov. That is how, one August afternoon, Grandpa and I found Dave and Paul standing at our doorstep.

Chapter 8

A New Life

Teplice-Sanov was a beautiful, quiet resort town, with tree-lined streets and lush green parks in the middle. We could not have picked a nicer place to settle down. It was hospitable to Jews, so, when we arrived, there was already a small Jewish community that was growing every day. Grandpa's friend was true to his word; after a short stay with him, we got our own apartment. And what a large, elegant apartment! Four fully-furnished rooms, complete with linen, bedding, dishes, china, pictures, and a piano. It was on the second floor of a luxury apartment house, with a balcony overlooking one of the parks with a public swimming pool and a bandstand where concerts were held on summer afternoons.

Of course, we knew quite well that all this had belonged to someone else, who may or may not have been a Nazi; someone who was forced to leave it all behind and allowed to take only what he or she could carry—exactly the same as it had been for the Jews. However, I did not find revenge sweet. I knew that if I allowed it to be an overriding factor in my life, I could become bitter and dehumanized.

Grandpa found a partner with whom to open a custom-tailoring shop that had been abandoned by its former German owner. Within a few weeks, they had a thriving business. Fabric—and everything else, for that matter—was available only on the black market; those who had connections prospered, and we were one of them.

Dave, then sixteen and among the youngest of the concentration camp survivors, went to work for Grandpa. Paul, who was eighteen, found work in a shoe factory.

What happened to Grandpa's other brothers? Someone who had been with Icu and Benyu in the concentration camp, and who had been liberated with them, told us they should be coming home any day. But they never made it. What happened?

Maybe they just gave up. Maybe they were ill and did not meet a compassionate commander. Maybe they were too timid to demand help. Who knows? In those times, life hung not even by a thread, but by a thread spun by a spider—never meant to hold a human being.

Teplice-Sanov and its environs were in many ways different from the town and the region I came from. Teplice and its people were much more sophisticated and cosmopolitan. We were only a two-hour train ride from Prague, where we would go often. The whole region was dotted with heavy industry, so the people were generally prosperous. Teplice-Sanov had one drawback: there was very little farming. Therefore, everything had to be shipped in and food was very scarce that fall and winter. Everything was rationed, even milk: one cup a day for people under twenty. Meat and eggs were almost nonexistent.

Buying food on the black market was a hit-and-miss affair. You did not necessarily buy what you wanted or needed; you bought what was available. For instance, one day Grandpa cornered the cream of wheat market. We cooked cream of wheat in so many ways for breakfast, lunch, and dinner, we could have written a cookbook on the many ways of serving that cereal.

Besides the black market, we had two other sources that kept us well nourished: old Mrs. Cuprinka from Lekard (who had hidden me in her home) would mail us crates of eggs, packed in straw and sawdust. At least half would survive the trip. Of course, some would break and many would crack. With the broken eggs, though, Paul and I would bake cakes. And so we had our much-needed protein.

Our other source of nourishment was real manna from heaven—packages from the U.S.A. Once a month, the local Jewish center would receive a food shipment—I think from the Hebrew Immigration Aid Society (H.I.A.S.)—and it would be distributed equally among all the Jewish families. I, as an expectant mother, got a double ration of powdered milk and eggs, spam, sardines, coffee, tea, sugar, canned fruit, even fresh grapefruits. These were luxuries that no money could buy.

Our baby was due in a short time, and we did not have as much as a diaper. Nowhere could one be had. No money could buy a layette and we certainly could not borrow one , as no one we knew had a baby. One day, the man at the Jewish center handed me a letter which I was to take to a warehouse. When I walked into that warehouse, I walked into baby heaven. It was full of baby clothes the likes of which I had never seen: little kimonos, nightgowns, sweaters, hats, knitted outfits, cotton outfits, booties, diapers, blankets. Nothing was for sale; it all belonged to an American Jewish organization and I was to have my pick of anything I wanted—as much as I could carry away!

And then Eva was born. She was the first Jewish child to be born in that whole region. She was the best-dressed little girl, the prettiest and the sweetest. To complete our happiness, we were finally able to get in touch with my sister Lenke in London.

Immediately upon liberation, I had sent telegrams and letters through the International Red Cross (the organization had acted as a go-between for families separated by the war) to find whoever had survived from my family, but to no avail. All I had was Lenke's address in Manchester, which I had memorized when I left home. But both Lenke and my cousin had left Manchester and the Red Cross could not locate them. But once again the tom-tom drums came to our aid. Someone who knew me met a cousin of ours in Israel, who notified Lenke. Naturally, the prettiest baby clothing arrived by mail from London, together with offers of assistance. But, by that time, we were firmly entrenched. We were doing well socially and financially. Our family was expanding too: my brother Miksa returned from the concentration camp, where he had lost his wife and two children, and came to live with us. We engaged the services of a lady who became our chief cook and bottle washer. This gave me a chance to devote my time to Eva and pine away for America. No matter how happy and successful we were, we all yearned to go to America. We were desperately searching for roots. The European soil was too saturated with the blood of our loved ones and dotted with their unmarked graves to be the place to put down roots. I think that was the primary reason we wanted to get away as far as we could. Of course, America represented Utopia to us. It held out the promise of a land full of riches, of justice, of opportunity, but mainly of a land unscarred by war. Besides, Grandpa's brother Sol and sister Roslyn and their families were in America. Family to us represented stability.

We were among the first to receive an affidavit, a letter of guarantee that someone will ensure your support if you immigrate to America. It was sent to us by uncle Sol. He obtained affidavits for all of Grandpa's family and all of his wife's surviving relatives. Grandpa's cousin Henry Hassenfeld of Providence, Rhode Island, the founder of Hasbro Toys, was responsible for our affidavit. In May, 1946, when Eva was eight months old, we went to Prague for our interview with the American consulate. We passed our interview and physical examinations and our papers were declared in order. They congratulated us and welcomed us aboard. We were told to leave our passports and pick up our visas the following week.

When we returned to the consulate the following week, they dropped a bombshell: with this being only the beginning of the post-war immigration, the Embassy staff had not previously been aware of all the nuances of the immigration laws. As it turned out, while Eva and I, who were born in Czechoslovakia, could have our visas the next day, Grandpa, because he was born in Poland, had to be admitted to the U.S. under the Polish quota and the Polish quota was already closed. This was the case even though Grandpa had left Poland with his family when he was six months old. Of course, Grandpa and I refused to be separated, so I did not exercise my option to receive a visa.

Soon, however, our extended family began to split up. Dave and Paul left for Germany to join Joe, now married to Carol, his first wife, and living in a displaced person's (D.P.) camp. Thanks to the immigration quotas, thousands of Eastern European Jews who had survived years in the Warsaw Ghetto and Auschwitz, were forced to languish in Germany in D.P. camps, some for as long as four years, awaiting their chances to go to America.

We, on the other hand, for the first time in our entire lives were alone in our own apartment.

Grandpa remained unable to get a visa to America. We wanted very much to visit Lenke in London, but the British also refused to give all three of us even visitor's visas. They were afraid that since "we had no compelling ties in Czechoslovakia," we would stay in England. After we received a few refusals, we realized that there was no alternative: Eva and I would have to go alone.

There is a little larceny in all of us and I am no exception. Now I will tell you the story of your grandma, the smuggler.

We knew that some people were making a lot of money smuggling Czechoslovakian crystal, garnet jewelry, and simulated pearls out of the country. So I decided that, just once, I would veer off the straight and narrow. Since there is no school for smuggling and you just don't go up to someone and ask "By the way, how do you smuggle merchandise in and out of the country?", we played it by ear and devised our own plans. I figured, since this was probably the only time I would do this sort of thing, that in order to make it pay, I ought to do it big! We bought out almost the entire inventory of crystal and jewelry at the store—wine sets, liquor sets, cake plates and platters by the dozen. The store owner came home with us to pack all the merchandise. We ended up with two big suitcases full of crystal and jewelry. The store owner brought with him a custom's officer who, for a bribe, sealed the valises and assured me that no one would open them. What he neglected to tell me was that those seals were worth "*bobkes*" out of the country. And I was allowed to take only one piece of crystal and one piece of jewelry out of Czechoslovakia.

Armed with two suitcases of contraband, one small suitcase containing our clothing, and a two-and-a-half-year-old child, I boarded the train to the West.

The enormity of my folly hit me as soon as we reached the border, when the train stopped and a group of customs officers boarded the train. In pairs, they inspected every compartment. When they reached our compartment and I saw their faces, my heart sank. They glanced at me, my papers, and my luggage and wished me a happy journey! Then they turned to the Polish Jew sitting next to me. He seemed nervous when they inspected his passport, so they asked him to follow them down the train. As he was leaving, he slipped something into the ashtray and motioned for me to keep quiet. I was too scared to move. After a while, he came back and the train pulled out. As it reached the border, he reached into the ashtray and pulled out a triple-strand necklace of cultured pearls and explained how lucky he was that they did not find it on him when they searched him. Because he was a man, he was not allowed to take any jewelry out of the country and he would have been jailed for smuggling. I, meanwhile, had dozens of necklaces in my suitcase. I knew I had to find a way out or I'd be done for. As I looked down the train, I noticed that almost the whole car was filled with peasant women. They were all going to America. When we reached the Belgian border, the train screeched to a halt and we were all ordered to get off the train with our luggage. I protested that my luggage was too heavy, but to no avail. The courteous, but firm customs officer assured me that my luggage had to be inspected and he would get help to take it down. I stood there in the custom's office with my heart in my shoes, visions of jail in a foreign land filled my mind. Just as the officer reached for the seal, I suddenly noticed that none of the peasants had gotten off the train. "Wait," I said. "Why aren't you searching their luggage?" I asked pointing to the peasants.

"Because they are in transit: they have tickets to America," he said.

"I am in transit too," I exclaimed. And with that I pulled out my ticket to London.

With apologies, he put back my luggage and we were off. But I was still not home free. I had to get into England. Realizing that my ticket to salvation was the peasants, I befriended them. They were all going to their husbands and fathers, who were in the U.S. They were sailing with the Cunard line from London. When we got to Belgium, they were met by a Cunard agent and, all together, boarded the ferry to Southampton. None of them spoke anything but Czech, so I, with my German and a little English, became their spokesman, the Cunard agent entrusted me with their guidance. After the most horribly choppy ferry ride, we arrived in Southampton. I got a few porters for our luggage. I put mine on the bottom and, when we reached the English customs officers, I said, "We are in transit." He said, "Show me your tickets." I turned to the women and in Czech asked for their tickets. Thirty steamboat tickets appeared, he put a cross mark on our luggage, and I was really home free!

Aunt Lenke, who was waiting for me at the dock in Southampton, tells the story of that day:

> Everyone got off the ferry and Rae was nowhere to be seen. When I asked someone about her, I was told that everyone had gotten off except a group of peasants. And there comes my sister followed by thirty peasant women in their costumes and *babuskas*!

Finally, we arrived at Lenke's house. When I opened my valises, Lenke and her husband Shaye could not believe their eyes. But there it was. I had not been caught. And shortly thereafter, I sold all that loot for about a thousand pounds, which was a small fortune then. I had spending money while I was in London! I also sent some home to Grandpa. (When Grandpa and I finally reached Canada, we furnished our entire apartment from that money.)

Our visit had been scheduled to last two weeks. We stayed for six months. It was a bittersweet visit from beginning to end. We rejoiced in each other and our respective families; we cried and talked endlessly about those of our loved ones that did not make it. Aunt Lenke and Uncle Shaye were very generous and loving. Once again, I was in a family setting. Her children reminded me of my other little nieces and nephews who had perished in Auschwitz. Shaye had brothers and many cousins with large families. They all lived close to each other and Friday night family visits became the norm. I had the feeling that, finally, I had come home. That feeling lasts to this day: when I feel down and homesick, I visit Lenke. In her and her children, I see everyone I have loved and lost.

Uncle Shaye was a renaissance man. Handsome, with a perpetual smile and laughing eyes, he was witty and wise. He had great business acumen, coupled with honesty and integrity. He had a great zest for life and took delight in anything and everything. Uncle Shaye was the only truly religious man I have ever met. He had an unwavering belief in God and an uncompromising view of good and evil. He was a very generous man, who did not preach religion, but practiced it to the letter of the law. Wherever he saw financial need, he corrected it. If he saw suffering, he helped to alleviate it. Countless people in London owe their financial success to him. He gave people a start in business; he raised the status of orphans; he arranged and paid for weddings people could not afford.

He and my sister led an exemplary life. Theirs was an open house, where every downtrodden person was welcomed.

The voice of my mother would echo in my ears: "We have to save her (meaning me) for Lenke."

I often wondered about fate, about why was I spared when others perished. But I was never happier that I was spared than when I lived with Lenke and Shaye. I considered myself privileged to be there. I knew how proud my mother would have been. I felt like a conduit: they all would see the family we lost through me and I would feel my mother's presence beside me when I was with them.

But this euphoria was short-lived. A great tragedy befell my country, which had a catastrophic effect on us. The democratically elected and beloved President Jan Masaryk, son of Thomas Masaryk, was assassinated and a Moscow-backed communist regime took over. The official version was that the President had jumped out of his office window. The unofficial and true version was that he was pushed out. The overthrow had far reaching effects. The borders were closed and no one was allowed out of the country. Many people were arrested at the slightest suspicion of having any connection with the West. Everyone advised Grandpa not to allow us to come home, since we had left the country only two days before the assassination. Not too many people visited the West in those days, and they were afraid that, if I returned, I might fall under suspicion and be arrested. We also felt that one man alone might find it easier to leave the country.

Many frantic letters and telegrams followed. Eva, although she felt at home with her cousins (who were her age), spoke English fluently by then and loved London dearly, missed Grandpa so very much that she cried herself to sleep every night. "I want my daddy," she would cry. I wanted him, too, but, at times, the situation seemed hopeless. The Polish quota was still closed and the U.S. Counsel would not make any allowances. Visas to smaller South American countries, like Costa Rica and Paraguay, were being peddled and Grandpa tried to get one, without success. We all decided that we would ask the U.S. consulate to send our papers to London, so that Eva and I could go to the U.S. alone. In doing so, we were assured that in a few weeks, we would have our visas. Meanwhile, we felt that a visit to the British Home Office was in order, since my visitor's visa had expired. We were looking for sympathetic assistance. The man who interviewed us could not have been more charming and sympathetic to our plight. He assured me that he would assist me in every way he could. Well, as for British sympathy and assistance. . . . The next day, I received a telegram from the British Home Office that read, "Madam, kindly leave the country within forty-eight hours!"

Armed with a basketful of Eva's favorite cereals, concentrated orange juice, home-baked cupcakes, and all the other goodies that Eva had gotten used to, and amid tearful farewells, we were set adrift in Europe. We were just two more of the truly homeless displaced persons.

We headed straight for Germany to join Grandpa's brothers Joe, Dave, and Paul, who were in Bad-Reichenhal. We were received with the same loving, generous hospitality. Whatever they had, they willingly shared with us. But what they had to offer was a far cry from what we had had before.

Lenke lived in a private house with a large garden, where the children played on swings and bicycles. We had a large private bed/sitting room with a fireplace all to ourselves.

Grandpa's brothers, in contrast, lived in converted army barracks that served as a D.P. camp for thousands of East European Jews of every nationality. Some had been there three or four years already. People met and got married there; children were born and raised there. To compensate for other things, children were allowed to be bratty and undisciplined. I recall watching one mother walking toward the corridor with a cup of cooked cereal in her hand, following a toddler; every time the child stopped, she shoved a spoonful of food in its mouth. They finished in the washroom.

Joe, his wife, and a French poodle lived in one small room, with two beds, one closet, and a Bunsen burner. The camp was filled to capacity, so we shared that room with them. The life they led was typical of the post-war refugees: a kind of limbo, suspended from the work-a-day world. It was a world of contrast and contradiction. In post-war Germany, food was scarce and the stores were empty. Yet, people ate well and were well dressed. Everyone was wheeling and dealing in the black market and all kinds of shady businesses. Outside the camp, in makeshift restaurants and cafés, people would socialize, dressed in their one set of finery. They were like groupies following each other.

Eva and Joe's little dog were inseparable. Together they became the pets of their numerous friends, who spoiled both of them rotten. The cereals and orange juice ran out, but in that world, if you ran out of orange juice, you offered champagne.

I must tell you about one incident which illustrates what a reunion site the D.P. camps proved to be. Joe's wife, Carol, took me to see some friends of hers from Budapest—in her words, "very rich and sophisticated" people. One look at the husband and I knew I had met him before. I kept asking him, "Have we met before, maybe in Budapest or Rumania, or London or Uzhorod?" He kept responding with a very positive "No." I kept staring at him. I knew I knew him; I just could not place him. He stared back at me, seeing that flicker of recognition in my eyes. Then, suddenly, he asked me to follow him outside, where he fell into my arms, calling me by a Russian name he had given me in Uzhorod. He was one of the Russian Jewish soldiers who had become my friend there! He used to stop by our tailoring shop. We'd speak Yiddish and sing Yiddish songs together. He had been very fond of vodka and I remember him lying drunk in the gutter at our wedding and being arrested the next morning because someone had stolen his gun. He had been the one who told us to leave Uzhorod.

He told me that he had been unable to face going back to Russia, so he defected and assumed a new identity. No one, not even his wife, knew about the old one.

As soon as we had arrived at the D.P. camp, we notified Grandpa, but we did not hear from him during the three weeks we were there. It was as if he had disappeared from the face of the earth. Then, one Sunday morning, while we were all gathered together and Joe was showing a piece of Meisen porcelain to an American couple, the doors opened and there stood Grandpa, with two small valises in his hand!

Words cannot describe the ensuing pandemonium. Tears of joy, of happiness, of relief began to flow. Six months of hopelessness, of waiting, of yearning came to an end in one split second. We all took turns hugging and kissing him, touching him to make sure he was real; only Eva stayed away when I told her to go to Daddy. She said, "I want my other Daddy." She did not recognize Grandpa. Eva had also forgotten the Czech language, so she and Grandpa could not communicate with one another.

The Czech and Hungarian languages had become part of our past by then; we spoke in English, the language of the future. But Grandpa could not speak it! So, we adopted the language of transition—Yiddish. Because the D.P. camps were such a melting pot of people and languages from so many countries, Yiddish had become the common denominator. Eva understood a little and began to talk with Grandpa in Yiddish.

But how did Grandpa come to join us? It was 1948. Israel was waging its War of Independence. The Haganah, Israel's underground army, was recruiting mostly single, Jewish men from Poland, Hungary, and Rumania. With the official sanction of the pro-Israel Czech government, the Haganah had been taking these men through Prague to Israel. There was one stipulation, which was scrupulously adhered to: Czech citizens could not be among them. When Grandpa had heard that we were in the D.P. camp in Germany, he became desperate. He threw away all of his papers, anything that could identify him. He cut out the labels from his clothes. He gave his house keys to one friend and the keys to the shop to another. He packed two small suitcases and contacted the Haganah. He told the soldiers he was Hungarian and they agreed to take him. With a group of other men, he thus came to Germany. Once in safe territory, he disappeared from the group and miraculously appeared on our doorstep.

We stayed in Germany for two months. It was summertime and one of Joe's friends had a car, so we explored the beautiful Bavarian mountains and countryside. But soon we saw that this kind of aimless life was not for us. We found a man whose shady "business specialty" was taking refugees across the French border. The fee was one hundred dollars, a fortune in post-war Germany, but we paid it. Joined by a grouchy, old Polish Jew (who had probably lost his family in Auschwitz and obviously did not like children) and one other person, we, the smuggler, and his driver started out on our journey to Paris, France. Five of us sat in the back of the car. We hadn't even considered the consequences of being caught. Still it was a frightening venture. Even if we made it, we did not know a soul in Paris and did not speak a word of French. In those days we knew as much about French culture as I know today about the moon!

We stopped about one hour's drive from the border at a farmhouse. About midnight, we headed toward our destination. We arrived at what we imagined to be the border. The smuggler went out and came back after a few minutes with bad news: his contact was not on duty that night. So we had to go back to the farmhouse and try again the next night. We spent that night and the next day in a bedroom with one big bed. Eva clung to us for dear life, but asked no questions. She was a trooper by then.

What I remember most about that trip, besides the numbing fear, are that grouchy old man's smelly feet and the friendly, beckoning lights behind the laced-curtained windows of the country homes we had passed along the way. It had been my first car ride ever through a darkened countryside. Oh, how I envied those people sleeping snuggled up with their loved ones, behind the safety of those lights!

On our second try the next night, we made it. We stopped in a small town in Alsace-Lorraine and then were off to Paris. Once in Paris, the smuggler led us to a hotel where he said we could stay for two days and nights. After we paid him, he exchanged our dollars for francs and disappeared. The first thing we wanted to do was notify our loved ones in England and Germany that we had arrived safely. It took us the whole afternoon to get to the post office (which turned out to be two blocks away). We must have stopped twenty people on the way to ask directions. We spoke a babel of languages—English, German, Yiddish, Czech, Hungarian—but the rapid French replies left us bewildered. It was thanks to the efforts of kind and patient people and hand gestures that we finally accomplished our mission.

The next day brought a new ordeal. We traveled to police headquarters, the "Prefecture Du Police," which was one hour's ride from us. We announced our presence as political refugees and were issued permits to stay in the country temporarily. There were two stipulations: we could not work or engage in commerce and we had to report to the police once a month. When we obtained visas from any country that could accept us as immigrants, we would be issued special "stateless passports." So, now, we were officially in limbo!

The next morning, while Eva and I were still asleep, Grandpa disappeared. Hours later, he came back elated. "I found a beautiful apartment in a "Chamber Meuble," he announced. "How? Where? How did you speak? How did you know how much they wanted?". . . I asked. Grandpa told us he had walked from hotel to hotel and had spoken with his hands until someone understood. When one woman agreed to show him a room, he opened his wad of bills and started to peel them off. When she motioned him to stop, he did.

Grandpa had said an apartment, but it was really one large, luxurious room in a hotel. It had one double bed in it, where the three of us slept; a large armoire, where we stored the dishes and groceries we bought; and a bidet, which we covered with a piece of lumber and a Bunsen burner. We stayed in that hotel for one year. It turned out to be one of the happiest years of our lives. It was far too expensive for us and for most other refugees we met, but that did not bother Grandpa. Undaunted, he started to walk again, this time from tailor shop to tailor shop, till he found a Yiddish-speaking custom tailor who, it turned out, was praying for a man like Grandpa. He procured working papers for him and became our friend and mentor. With Grandpa's help, they branched out into ready-to-wear clothing, and before we left he offered Grandpa a partnership. We were the only refugee family that had a father who worked and was not on public assistance.

Our hotel was ideally situated: Rue De Martyr, across from the Pigalle and just near the "Sacre Coeur." We were within walking distance of Montmarte, the Moulin Rouge—all the fun and exciting places. We walked day and night. We crisscrossed Paris on foot, by metro, and by bus. We planned ahead and, every weekend, the three of us would explore another part of town. We knew every park, every historic site, every tourist attraction. We picnicked in the "Bois de Boulougne" and "Versailles" and loved every minute of it.

The hotel proved to be a microcosm of life. The owner and concierge of the five-story walk-up was the widow of a French army officer—a middle-aged Parisian matron with flaming red hair and over-rouged cheeks. Like a reigning queen, she would hold court in her salon with her young and handsome Tunisian lover by her side. Two happy-go-lucky secretaries occupied one apartment on our floor. One of them, Betina, spoke English fluently. They became our friends and French teachers. Next door to us lived a bedridden woman with one baby and a dark-eyed little girl about Eva's age, who would sometimes come out and play with her. We had never met the parents until, one day, I was in the hallway with the children when the father came home. He was also Tunisian (there were many Tunisian refugees in Paris then). He stopped to talk to his child and, at that moment, Grandpa came along carrying a Jewish newspaper under his arm. Noticing the paper, the Tunisian wildly embraced both of us, exclaiming "*Amchu, Amchu!*" In Hebrew, *Amchu* means "nation." He pointed to us and then to himself. "You, me, *Amchu,*" he said and dragged us into the room, where his ailing child and wife lay. We became close friends. Though we had come from different backgrounds and could not communicate, we were kindred spirits, both refugees and Jews.

Above the fifth floor was an attic with a slanted ceiling and one window opening to the rooftop. There a woman named Madeline lived with her daughter, Colette. Madeline had seen

better days. As a pretty young girl, fresh from the farm, she had
been kept by men of means. The last "Monsieur" she had lived
with in her apartment, she told me, abandoned her when she
became pregnant. So she and her child were relegated to the
attic. I do not know what she did for a living, but often Colette
would come in and say she couldn't go home yet "because a
monsieur is with Mama."

In spite of the language barrier, Colette and Eva, two not-
quite three-year-olds, became best friends and constant com-
panions. When Colette would go off to nursery school (which
the French provided, free of charge, for every child), Eva would
cry. So, one day, we brought her a lunch box and took her to the
door of the nursery. She said, "Good-bye, Mama," and she was
off to school too!

With my husband off to work and my child off to school, I
settled into the role of Parisian housewife and loved it. I became
familiar with the merchants and vendors on the street. They all
became my tutors. Whenever I pointed to something I wanted
to purchase, they told me the name of it in French. The hardest
part was not being understood in a store where what I wanted
was not on display. There usually followed a few minutes of
misunderstanding, sometimes embarrassing *double entendres*,
and jokes at my expense. About three or four weeks after Eva
started nursery school, the three of us were in a store. The merchants were simply not on the same wavelength as we were and
we were not making any headway. Then, out of the blue, Eva
turned to me and said, "The man says. . . ." She proceeded to interpret for me in English, then for Grandpa in Yiddish. Then she
turned to the man and, in fluent French, told him what we
wanted. She became the official interpreter for us and the other
refugees we had met by then.

We met many Hungarian refugees in Paris and had a great social life. While in the park one day, I met a girl I had gone to
school with! She, her husband, and little boy were also on their
way to America. The place they were staying in was horrible, so
for a while they moved into our hotel.

We weren't so alone anymore. And then another couple we
knew from Teplice-Sanov moved in on the fifth floor. Their
apartment was cheaper and not so nicely furnished, but it had a
sink and a portable gas range in the kitchen. In those days, that
qualified the kitchen as a luxury kitchen. The woman and her

husband were both tailors and worked during the day. In exchange for finding them customers, she let me cook my meals in
her kitchen, with one condition: I could not keep anything of
mine there. So, every day, I *shlepped* everything I needed—both
dishes and food—from my second-floor room to the fifth floor.
If I forgot something, which I did often, I ran down for it. My
neighbors used to say, "There runs the mad Hungarian for her
paprika." Nevertheless, I cooked food for many a dinner party
there. And, almost every day, we had one or two single men
from our hometown over for dinner. Then the couple left for the
U.S. and we inherited their apartment!

About our status: after we had arrived in Paris, we were
notified that Eva's and my visas were now ready—but in London. So, we had all our papers transferred to Paris and started
the proceedings again. Because a few years had elapsed, we had
to have new medical examinations.

Our misspent youth had left some scars on our lungs, which
showed up on X-rays. We knew these scars could lead a doctor
to refuse us visas on medical grounds. It was left to his discre-
tion. The doctor in Prague was a kindly man and chose to over-
look the scars. The doctor in Paris, however, was a notoriously
mean man who went strictly by the book. So we knew we could
not take a chance.

A couple we knew well, the same age and build as we, who
had already passed the physical and gotten their visas, agreed to
stand in for us. We explained to Eva that, for this particular
afternoon only, they would be her mommy and daddy. We all
walked into the waiting room. Eva looked at me with those all-
knowing eyes, calmly took their hands and said, "Come,
Mommy and Daddy." The three of them walked into the
doctor's office. For the doctor's benefit, Eva loudly addressed
them as "Mommy and Daddy" three more times. We passed
with flying colors, but the Polish quota remained closed. One by
one, our friends were heading for the U.S. We were among the
few who were left behind.

I, like George Gershwin, "loved Paris in the springtime." The
street corners were awash with lilies of the valley and violets,
which the street vendors were selling. The chestnut trees were in
full bloom and so was I. I was expecting again. First there was a
surge of happiness (we did want a large family). But then came
despair. After all, we were four years older, wiser, and a little

world-weary. The question was not so much how, but where. Where would I have the baby? In the one room, with the one bed? The U.S. Consul was very sympathetic, but not much help. Grandpa was distraught, but I could hear my mother's voice as she used to say, "Every child brings its own *mazel*." We wrote to Uncle Sol, who had sent us the original papers, and, one morning, when I was particularly dejected and blue, a letter arrived from him that opened the door for us to go to Canada.

The Statute of Limitations is up, so I will, dear children, tell it as it was, no holds barred. There was a go-between who, for a fee, obtained visas to Canada. Any blood relative could sponsor you, be it sister, brother or cousin. Many people, for a fee, became cousins. We found such a man, whose name coincided with ours, except for the fact that Grandpa's mother's maiden name had to be changed to his name. With this change, they would become stepbrothers. However, this transaction would mean, that we could never come to the U.S. because Grandpa's rightful mother's name was registered there. (The U.S. was the only place where it was registered, since we had no passports.) This dilemma made us hesitate.

Then Aunt Lenke came to visit us. She was appalled at my appearance. Just as when I was carrying Eva, the beginning of my pregnancy was very difficult. I could not hold down food; I was constantly vomiting. I became dehydrated and she insisted that I go to the hospital. Completely debilitated, I ended up having to stay there for two weeks. Lenke had to return to London and we had no one to care for Eva. So, every morning, Grandpa would take Eva to the nursery. Colette's mother would pick up the children at 5 o'clock and keep Eva at her house until Grandpa came home from work and visiting me. One night, Grandpa came home to find Colette's door locked. Finally, her mother came home, a little under the influence, with no girls! Grandpa was frantic. Together they combed the streets for a long time, till they found the two three-year-olds, lunch boxes in hand, walking the streets of "Pigalli." It turned out that there had been "a monsieur with Mama." They had gone down to the bar to hoist a drink or two and forgot about the girls. Well, needless to say, Grandpa was scared out of his wits.

Besides that, the medical care, and the hospital care in particular, was notoriously bad in post-war Paris. The equipment was inadequate. The hospitals were dirty, understaffed, and short of supplies. Whatever else the Parisians' virtues, cleanliness was not one of them. When I got sick, Grandpa was cautioned not to put me in a public hospital. So I was staying in a private maternity clinic, where the care was horrendous anyway. What we saw there—the filth, the shortage of nurses, the women in labor screaming for hours before anyone paid attention to them—brought into sharp focus the fact that, being alone in this city, living in that hotel with no possible chance of an apartment, we could not have our baby in Paris!

Since we were unable to get any assurance that we would get U.S. visas in the near future, we applied for stateless passports (the ones where Grandpa's mother's name was changed), which would enable us to go to Canada. The die was cast. Good-bye forever, U.S., hello Canada.

What a send-off we had from Paris! The day before we left, the French people were celebrating Bastille Day. They were dancing in the streets all day and all night. Grandpa was out with Eva till the wee hours of the morning. The next day, we said a tearful good-bye to our Parisian friends and that glorious city. After sitting up all night in Le Havre's run-down, bombed-out waiting room, where you could see the stars through the broken roof, we finally set sail for Canada the next morning.

Chapter 9

Life in the New World

We sailed on the S.S. Scythia, not a great, majestic ship, but a hastily converted troop carrier in an ocean-going tub without much ballast. Ferrying the masses of refugees across the Atlantic was its last hurrah before being retired to the junkyard. We sailed "steerage class" in a large cavernous room lined with bunks. Families were separated by sex. As for food, all I remember is one meal in the common dining room, where we met another Hungarian couple. The rest is a blur. I was in my bed, retching through the whole crossing. I surely thought that I would lose the baby, but he held on for dear life. Eva and Grandpa fared better. They roamed the ship. Eva was the darling of everyone. Grandpa would come visit me during the day, coax me to eat, and try to cheer me up, but to no avail. I thought I would die.

But this too passed. Finally, we arrived at the dazzling Quebec port. The sun shone on gaily colored houses that seemed to be painted one on top of another on the mountainside. We came to a bright new world full of hopes and expectation; but the new world was very unkind to us.

First of all, we arrived during an unusual, smoldering heat wave. In all our lives, we had never experienced such humidity and heat. Still shaken from the boat ride, I boarded the train to Montreal, where we arrived late in the evening. Just as the ocean voyage is a blur in my mind, the welcome we received at the train station is indelibly etched in my mind.

We were met at the station by a representative of the Canadian Jewish Congress (CJC). Our passage had been paid for by IRO, an international rescue organization, and the IRO was notified of our arrival. I remember standing in the railroad station, the sweat pouring from us, my knees buckling under me, when he started to ask questions. Seeing us getting caught up in bureaucratic mumbo jumbo, I walked up to him and asked, "Please, could you first take us to our room, where we could get comfortable?" He threw his hands up in the air and exclaimed, "I don't understand you people. What are you coming here for? Just what do you think you will find here? Don't you understand that there is a medical convention on and all the hotels are booked?" I looked at him in disbelief.

For years, while crisscrossing Europe, I yearned for a land where my people, my brethren, would be spared the trauma and tragedies that we had endured. I visualized a place where I would be embraced, comforted, and helped. And here was this man, looking at me and my belly and the tired child at my side, saying he did not understand people like me.

I wish I could say that this was an isolated incident, but, in general, the Canadian Jews turned out to be uncaring and inhospitable. They regarded us as a threat to their own security. They looked upon us as barbarians who had to be taught the amenities, such as how to flush a toilet.

But back to that evening in the train station: The CJC representative finally took us to a hotel which had been paid for by the CJC for three nights. That was all the help we received from the Canadian Jewish community. The next day, while I lay in bed, dazed from the heat and exhaustion, putting wet compresses on my head and body, Grandpa went to the CJC office. They grilled him there to the point that he admitted to having relations in the U.S. They told him it was the duty of our relatives to help us and they refused us further assistance, other than to give Grandpa a newspaper in which to look for furnished rooms.

And Grandpa began his search. When he told a prospective landlord that his wife was expecting a baby, the landlord refused to rent him the room. We couldn't turn to Joe, Paul or Dave for help; they had arrived in New York just three months before. They, themselves, were receiving assistance from HIAS (which, by the way, was compassionate, caring, and sufficient for getting a foothold in this new land). The only people we could turn to for help were the Lichtigs. They had rented a house from some people who had left Montreal for the summer and we moved in with them. The heat was relentless. It lasted for three weeks. We tried again to get an affordable apartment of our own, without success.

Older, low-rent apartments were unavailable. Even if one could be found, the key money was prohibitive. There was a huge building boom, and rows of new apartments had just been built on the edge of town, but the rents were $90 for a one-bedroom and $110 for a two-bedroom apartment—a lot of money at that time. The Lichtigs and some other refugees managed to rent these apartment. They were all businessmen, some of them older than we and most of them with more money. Joe, Carol, and Sol came to visit us, but were not able to advise us as to what to do.

Grandpa landed many job offers, but no one would commit himself to naming a salary. Still, we were not worried. Why should we be? We had been all over the world and no one had taken advantage of us. Grandpa was a master in his trade, hardworking and diligent. One employer was particularly persuasive: "Just take care of your family; get them settled," he said, "and come to work for me. You will make a living." We finally succumbed to the temptation. We signed a two-year lease for a one-bedroom apartment at a rent of ninety dollars a month.

Ever since I had gotten married—and even before—I had dreamt of the day when I would stand by the door of my own apartment and watch my new furniture being delivered. Well, it finally happened. There I stood at the door of the most luxurious one-bedroom apartment, beautiful beyond my wildest dreams: a great big Hollywood kitchen with all new appliances; a colorfully tiled bathroom; and big, sunny rooms. And the furniture! Hopeful fools that we were, we fully furnished the place with the cash we had gotten from selling that London crystal. We bought a maroon-brocaded and carved living room set, complete with lamps and a standing ashtray, even though we did not smoke. We were ready to be the perfect hosts to the guests we were going to entertain.

Grandpa started his new job. The workers there were paid every two weeks. Every time Grandpa approached the boss about his wages, the boss patted his shoulder and told him not to worry. By the end of the two weeks, one of Grandpa's shoulders was lower than the other, but not lower than his wages! He was paid twenty-five dollars a week. A rude awakening and a new lesson to be learned: Canadian Jews do take advantage of newcomers. The whole garment industry was in Jewish hands. Union places did pay better, but only union members could work in union shops and it was difficult to get into the union. So, non-union shops, like the one Grandpa worked in, had a ready supply of cheap labor. Grandpa worked overtime and brought work home with him. In addition, he did alterations and pressed cloth for all our friends, but still he could not cover expenses.

Poverty cannot always be measured by outward appearances. We wore custom-made clothes from Paris; I had alligator bags. Our apartment was beautifully furnished. But with all our reserve funds gone, we were dirt poor. Having neither money nor health insurance when Jackie was born, I was just another ward patient to the unknown doctor who delivered him. I was treated as "just another barbarian refugee." (That was how my fellow Polish survivors and I were regarded: barbarians who still nursed their babies.) Grandpa did not have enough money in his possession to pay for the most meager refreshments at the *bris.* There was no kindly Jewish organization to supply a layette. But we had many good and generous friends, who supplied the bare necessities. Once again, my child was the first to be born to one of us in this new land. He was the most beautiful baby, with white translucent skin and bronze/red wavy hair. He looked like a porcelain doll. We didn't even have a crib for him when we got home. For weeks, he slept in one of the chest drawers. But he was king of the castle anyway and he loudly proclaimed that for everyone to hear. He was colicky and screamed day and night for months.

It would have been difficult for us to "keep up with the Joneses," except that the "Joneses" were hurting too. One by one, those with two-bedroom apartments took in a newly arrived couple. Women whose husbands went into business went to work in factories, supporting the household, while their businesses got established. Women with smaller children watched and fed the children of the working mothers.

We put a sofa bed into my beautiful living room and rented it to a bachelor brother of a friend of ours from Teplice-Sanov. The room and board we charged him covered our rent. It worked out fine for a while. The winter was long and harsh and we were homebound. I watched the children. Our boarder, who was a rabbinical student at the seminary, studied. But he must have been absent from school the day that one of the Ten Commandments was taught—the one that says, "Thou shalt not covet thy neighbor's wife." At first, his playful innuendos were only humiliating and degrading to me, but when he became bolder, we decided to let him go. It was a great blow to our pocketbook, so I began to watch two of our neighbor's little girls. Their parents started a pocketbook factory and so the mother was away full-time. Try as hard as we did, we could not make ends meet.

The only way we could get ahead would be for Grandpa to strike out on his own. There were many opportunities, but we were lacking capital. We saw no way to save up the money in the near future. We couldn't even pay our rent. The U.S., where beginnings were easier, and where we would have had the support of our family, was still closed to us. Then something happened which set my mind working—a real stroke of luck.

It was an early spring day. The snow was melting and the hilly streets and gutters were overflowing with water and mud. I went to do some errands with Eva at my side and Jackie in a small stroller. I do not remember why I had our passports with me (at that time they were only paper documents, not books), but somewhere on the way, I lost them. I knew Grandpa would be very angry with me (we were irritable those days and easily upset). All the way home, I was figuring out what I could say to cushion the blow. Then, like a flash of lightening, an idea hit me;it was so phenomenal that I ran home breathlessly. I hugged and kissed Grandpa and laughed and cried at the same time. "I lost the passports," I said. Grandpa thought I was off my rocker. "You lost the passports and you're so happy? You're nuts," he answered. "No, Harry, can't you see that I lost our passports, the only place where your mother is not really your mother?" I explained. Grandpa understood. We called the police and reported the passports missing. The next day, we received a call telling us that someone had found two documents where I had said I had lost mine. They looked like our passports, but were drenched in mud and were not legible. Armed with the policeman's number and the case number, we went to the U.S. consulate and told them about our lost passports. We asked them to have our papers forwarded from Paris. They advised us to go to a certain office and give the people there the police records. After they verified that our passports were really lost, we were issued new ones, this time with all the right relatives. We were almost home free. But the wheels at the Consulate ground slowly and we still were struggling to pay our rent.

We befriended the family of a man who had been in the forced labor camps with Grandpa. A nice, quiet couple, they had a three-year-old boy who got along well with our children. They were in the same boat as we were: they could not pay their rent. We seemed to be compatible in every way, so we decided that the answer for both of us was to move in together. We rented a two-bedroom apartment in a great big corner apartment house a little further out of town. It wasn't brand new but it was nice.

It didn't take long to realize that we had made a colossal mistake. The woman was a Jekyl and Hyde type. When her husband was home, she was all sweetness and light. When she was alone with that poor little boy, she was a basket case. For the smallest infraction, she would seat him on the kitchen table and keep him there for hours, often beating him with an electric rod. She would abuse him during the day, then soak him and bathe him before the husband came home. When we told the husband, the mother and child denied it. That child was both abused and brainwashed. I tried to keep out of the mother's way. The kid was another matter, however. He had to take out his rage on someone and that someone turned out to be my poor child. Jackie was about a year old then and had just started to walk. That kid would stalk him like a jungle cat lying in the grass. When Jackie took a few unsteady steps, he'd pounce on him or brush by him and make him fall. That mother and child made our lives hell.

Eva was in nursery school all day; she was picked up at nine in the morning and brought home at four in the afternoon. So I would stay out as much as I could. Luckily for us, it was summer. I'd spend time outside or visit one of my many friends. I dreaded going home. I was slowly losing control and could cope less and less. Then, one Sunday afternoon early in September, we were ready to go out with the children. The kid was being particularly obnoxious so I ran out of the house with our children and Grandpa was to follow. He came out to the balcony to see us off. I began pushing Jackie in the stroller, with Eva next to me, pulling her red wagon. We stepped off the curb and, simultaneously, I heard a blood-curdling shriek from Grandpa and the screech of an approaching car taking the curve. Eva fell. When I brought her to her feet, blood was pouring from her face. I surely thought that this was the end. Luckily, it turned out that the fender had hit her forehead and she had fallen away from the car. It had not gone over her. I will not dwell on the ensuing hysterics. Suffice it to say that her forehead was split open near her hairline and she got a slight concussion. She spent a few days in the hospital and then, miraculously, she was released as good as new.

Grandpa had seen the car coming and knew it would hit Eva, since the driver was taking the curve with such speed. We engaged a lawyer from the neighborhood. The man who had been driving the car was also from the neighborhood. Unbeknownst to us, he and the lawyer were good friends and belonged to the same shul. When we engaged the lawyer, he had told us he was sure we had a good case. The next day, gently but firmly, he advised us not to press charges. After all, this man had meant no harm to us, he said, being such an upright citizen, a doll manufacturer. Never mind the physical or emotional scars that our child might have. But he appealed to our consciences. Fools that we were, we didn't want to appear opportunistic to these high and mighty people, who looked down on us anyway. We signed away all further claims in exchange for one hundred dollars above the medical expenses and a Shirley Temple doll. This is the difference between being downtrodden and being well connected. When you are well connected, you can pay for and receive good advice; when you are down, you are on your own and you begin to doubt your judgment.

November was upon us and with it came the cold weather. We were homebound more and more—that neurotic woman, I, and the helpless little children. One morning, she went on a rampage. The little boy would not eat, so she had him on the table the whole morning, wielding that electric cord like a lion tamer in the circus. I was afraid if I stayed there long enough, we would both end up in the looney bin—she being ripe for it already and I slowly losing more of my cool.

When Grandpa came home that night, I was on the verge of a nervous breakdown. I raged and ranted, screaming for him to take me away from there. I was ready to go anywhere, as long as we could be alone. I threatened to leave him and the kids if we didn't leave. I know he took me seriously because, the next day, he took time off from work (a drastic measure for Grandpa) and, armed with the newspaper, looked for and found an apartment.

The only way I can explain the location and everything else about this new apartment is to tell you it was the equivalent of a three-family tenement on Delancey Street on the Lower East Side. The only difference was that the streets were much cleaner and the houses better kept. Our new home was a converted cold-water apartment with sort of railroadish rooms. But it was cheap and we were to be blissfully alone.

The day I was packing, "the kid" was annoying Jackie, so Jackie followed me as I went from room to room. As I shut the door to the room I was in at the moment, I accidently caught his little finger and cut off the tip of his pinky.

Jackie and I spent the morning crying in the emergency room. Once again, we had no private doctor, no insurance, and no connections. The intern on call discussed with us the difference between well-bred and controlled native patients and the hysterical immigrants. Yes, I certainly was hysterical that day, one of the worst in a long list of worst days in that worst period of my married life. I could not phone Grandpa because he was on a new job and I did not have his phone number.

When Grandpa came home that evening with the mover and saw that everything was not packed, he asked me why. My reply eliminated a few of our dishes. He ducked and we had less to pack. Around midnight we arrived at our new home. The landlords, a lovely old Russian Jewish couple, came up to welcome us with a home-baked cake and a pot of hot coffee. They were nice, simple people, who restored our faith in humanity. We left all our fancy friends behind in our old neighborhood and became good friends with the landlord's married daughter and her family, who lived in our building. Our children played together. Theirs was a closely knit family. Brothers and sisters often visited with the parents. We looked lovingly at all those aunts and uncles; ours were in New York—so near and yet so far.

And then I became pregnant again. At the first sign of pregnancy, I became sicker than ever. I could not look at or smell food. I could not take care of or feed my children. Grandpa could not stay home; he was barely able to eke out a living. So I would give Eva a piece of meat and send her to the landlady, who would cook it and fed her and Jackie. God bless her! She saved my life.

Suddenly it was time for us to move on. The Polish quota opened up, exactly five years after we had first applied. Though it had only been five years, it had seemed like ages.

Chapter 10

America

In January, 1951, we arrived at Grand Central Station in New York. I was twenty-five years old, world weary, mentally and physically debilitated, and I felt as old as Methuselah. We piled into Uncle Joe's awaiting car and off we went into the land of our dreams. But, somehow, the reality distorted my dream. The New York of my dreams, from all the movies I had seen, had bright lights, wide streets and handsome people. But here we were, on a murky, slushy, Sunday morning in January, driving home from the Forty-Second Street station under the West Side Highway on the ugliest, dirtiest street I had ever seen. And it did not get better further along in the ride.

We drove through the Bowery and the Lower East Side, through mind-boggling squalor. Then we crossed the Williamsburg Bridge to Brooklyn, which was even uglier and shoddier than the Manhattan we had just left. Broadway, under the elevated platform with the subway roaring by, had a row of almost dilapidated, ill kept houses and stores, matched only by the ill-kept people who roamed there. Two streets beyond Broadway was Grove Street. There stood four four-story walk-up apartment houses. In one of these was Joe's three-room apartment.

The neighborhood was definitely lower class. Joe and Carol moved into the living room and we took over their bedroom, staying there for three months.

The one thing that is essential to an immigrant, if he is to succeed in a new country, is to have self-induced amnesia. He must forget who he was, what he owned, and where he lived previously. If he continued to dwell on his past position, his wealth or his earlier station in life, he was doomed.

Inwardly, I cried. I mourned for all the beautiful cities I had left behind and for the lovely apartments that had been my homes. Like it or not, this was to be my home now. Armed with determination and high hopes, surrounded by loving family, I knew I could—and must—succeed.

Dave found a job for Grandpa on Fifty-Seventh Street in Manhattan in a custom-tailoring shop, where they made high-fashioned ladies' suits for high society—the Fords and the Rockefellers. Grandpa started to work immediately at an agreed upon salary of seventy-five dollars a week. At the end of the week, the boss handed him his paycheck and said, "Harry, you are a good craftsman; your work is just as excellent as that of men who have worked for me for years; I don't think it is fair for me to pay you less." The check was for eighty-five dollars. To us, it seemed like a fortune. Grandpa had never made more than fifty dollars a week in Canada. Besides the money, the words of praise helped heal the wounds to Grandpa's pride inflicted in Canada. But there is no greater blow to a man's pride than when his family is hurting because he cannot support them, especially a man with old-fashioned ideas and loyalties, as Grandpa had. His self-esteem had been at a low ebb.

Joe and Carol had many good friends and we were included in their circle. Carol was carefree and gay and that rubbed off on us. She loved to shop and took me with her for lunch in the city and on shopping sprees to S. Klein, her favorite haunt. I was not feeling well and was under medical care for awhile. Three weeks later, I had a miscarriage. Since we had no money or medical insurance, we borrowed four hundred dollars from Joe to cover the expenses.

Carol nursed me back to health and Joe could not do enough for us. They cared for the children as if they were their own. Every day, Joe would come home laden with cakes, fruit—everything and anything he thought we might want. He would not let us contribute any money to the household.

At the drop of a hat, Dave and Paul would come to visit and stay for dinner. We often visited with Roslyn and her family, too. Surrounded by a loving, caring family, we slowly recovered our strength and our spirits.

Three months later, Joe found us an apartment in one of the adjoining buildings. It was a crumby apartment over a bridal shop, with no windows in the bedroom, but we had no choice; we had to take our furniture out of storage.

After we had spent two months there, Joe finally succeeded in getting an apartment for us in the house next to his. It was a fourth-floor walk up, with four rooms and windows in the rear. Of the four apartments on our floor, three were occupied by Hungarian refugees. We were all in the same boat—struggling. Our children were more or less the same age. While we did not share many interests, there was enough to bind us together and we became friends. Eva was the oldest and so she was the caretaker. I think she was born reliable, responsible, and all knowing. Under her supervision, the children would play outside on the sidewalk with all the other children. You know the old adage, "The rich get rich and the poor get children." Every once in a while, they would ring my bell. I would go to my neighbor's front window and they would ask me to throw down this or that. Jackie would always ask for a glass of milk.

We celebrated birthday parties, Thanksgiving dinners, and Passover with our extended families, Roslyn's in-laws, uncles, aunts, and cousins too. We met Grandpa's uncles, aunts, and many children, who lived here in the States. And we met the many cousins' children as well.

I cannot pinpoint when it happened, but, as if a magic wand had touched us, the future began to look bright. We seemed to be in the mainstream, no longer on the outside. Sentimental as this may sound, I began to think of myself as an American. This was my country, flaws and warts and all. I began to see the possibilities here; we were sure our chance would come for a better life.

Joe bought an old '49 Packard and, on weekends, we would all pile in, meet Roslyn and her family, and go for picnics in a park or on the beach. We were a closely knit family then and everyone pitched in to help us. Roslyn bought new pots and pans for us and lent us money to buy a washing machine. Joe gave us a sewing machine. When my back went out (yes, my backaches go that far back) and I was bedridden for a few days, Paul stayed over, and cared for the children. We were not alone anymore.

Paul was engaged to be married. His future in-laws, the Schaffers, were financially comfortable people. They owned their own home, drove a nice car, and had a small bungalow colony. They were retired and spent their winters in Florida. They were able to educate their children and plan a big wedding for their daughter, sparing no expenses. I was surprised to find that all their money came from owning a cleaning store. Mrs.

Schaffer told me, with a twinkle in her blue eyes, "When I was younger, I worked side by side with my husband; now we are older and are enjoying ourselves side by side." I thought to myself, "This is for me. If they could do it, we could do it too." But first we had to have some capital.

Grandpa loved his job and his boss. His co-worker, Jerry, became a lifelong friend. But the work was seasonal; off-season, Grandpa would work in a cleaning store. He always held down two jobs, but still the income wasn't enough for us to save any money. Eva was in school and Jackie in a nursery school. I tried working in a clothing factory in the neighborhood. So, I don't know who hated the day more—Jackie at nursery school or me sitting by that sewing machine and mindlessly doing piecework. Jackie was small and, thank God, he did not feel duty bound to suppress his emotions. He protested loudly and I quit.

Then the fancy men's custom-tailoring shop next door to Grandpa's place needed another tailor to do alterations. Grandpa did not want to give up his job and go to work there, but the owner and he worked it out so that he could do the work at home. Whatever he brought home at night, if necessary he would bring it back on the next or the second morning. Night after night, week after week, Grandpa brought the work home on the subway. We would put the children to bed, clear the table, and, together, finish everything. We listened to the radio and wove our future. Those were special evenings for both of us. Sometimes, we worked half the night. Other times, when there was a bigger job to do, I would work in the afternoon. One day, I met one of my neighbors, a nice elderly lady, who lived below us, she asked, "Tell me, don't you people ever sleep?" I explained to her what we were doing. She said, "I guess you have to do what you have to do." She was right. And that was that. Throughout the year and a half we worked like that, we never cashed the week's paycheck. We did not want to be tempted to spend it. We opened a bank account and those checks went straight into the bank.

When we had saved two thousand dollars, just as we had planned, we began to look for a store of our own. We met a man named Kron. He was a rotund, short, kind gentleman with a big cigar (and a heart to match). He was a business broker who knew every cleaning store in Brooklyn. It was off-season and Grandpa was out of work. Kron would pick us up in his big

Cadillac and drive us around Brooklyn and Queens, patiently teaching us all he knew about cleaning stores (which was everything). He had owned one himself for years. This went on for three months.

We considered one or two stores, but either they were not in a neighborhood we would consider living in or cost too much money or were too great a risk. Mr. Kron gained our confidence; he earnestly wanted us to succeed. But we found nothing. Still, in the meanwhile, we got to know all about the business. Then Grandpa's season started and he went back to work. We said good-bye to Mr. Kron, we thought, till the next off-season. But one day, Mr. Kron called me, very excited. He said, "Be ready in one hour; I am picking you up." "But, Mr. Kron," I protested, "my husband is at work."

"Just be ready," he said. (This meant that I had to find a baby-sitter, but I had many good friends and so that was never a problem.)

When he picked me up, he told me he would talk to me first as a father, then as a broker.

"Mrs. Halpern," he said, "there are times to be the little woman, but this is not one of them. You should work together with your husband, but don't be afraid to make decisions on your own. You know as much about this business as he does (This was the first time anyone had talked to me "man-to-man.") "By now," he continued, "I know what you want and I have the perfect business for you. The reason I did not show it to you before is that another client of mine was negotiating for it and I never show a business to someone else while one client is considering it. This buyer checked out the business thoroughly, cased it, watched it for days from the outside, bargained and brought the price down, and negotiated a good lease from the landlord. This morning the owners called me, upset, because the buyer proposed to cut me out of the deal, to save the commission. They refused to do business with such dishonest people." Mr. Kron then drove me around the neighborhood. I never saw such palatial houses, such beautiful gardens, such wide streets. We stopped by the public school and by the temple—each about five blocks away.

The business really had everything we wanted. It had the best location—a big, airy, bright corner store, three blocks from the Narrows—and a well-dressed, well-heeled clientele. The owners were simple, honest people as we were. This was a well-established business, not a fly-by-night operation. The owners, three brothers, had decided to split up after eight years together, but that spot had been the home of a cleaning store for the last forty years. Although we sold the business years ago, it is still a thriving cleaning store today! I asked a few questions, but I knew all the answers. Mr. Kron had filled me in on everything. It all added up. The price was five thousand dollars, firm, already prenegotiated by the other buyer.

I met the landlord and got very good vibes. These were all honest, simple people. Everything seemed to fall into place. Mr. Kron and I went for a ride again. He told me to trust him and my judgment and I did. We went back to the store. I made an offer, on paper, in Grandpa's name. We had until the morning to change our minds.

Grandpa loved everything he heard, but said he had to go to his job to give notice and collect his scissors. We could not afford to hire our own lawyer, so we used the seller's lawyer. Mr. Kron assured us he would look out for our interests, and he did. Grandpa arrived with his scissors, looked around, the papers were drawn up and Grandpa signed them. We had two thousand dollars of our own and had borrowed the rest from our relatives, mainly from Emery, Roslyn's husband. In the middle of the contract signing, we realized our funds were insufficient. The lawyer, the broker, the seller, and the landlord all took I.O.U.s. We owed for utilities deposits; everything else they trusted us on. The next day, the man who had originally wanted to buy the store offered us a one-thousand dollar profit to sell it to him. We didn't.

Easter week was our first week in business. We had a hand-cranked antique cash register, which made a ringing sound when you turned it. It continued to ring all week. We could not believe our good luck. Our customers were the nicest people, with names like Jabara, Mammary and Caraba, names we had never heard before. They all seemed genuinely happy for us and wished us good luck. When we sold the business twenty-eight years later, we still had most of those customers and their children.

At first, it seemed that we had bitten off more than we could chew. Grandpa had worked all his life, but at a slow pace, doing careful custom-tailoring. In a cleaning store, you have to do ten things at the same time, fast and well. It was back breaking work. Grandpa would often put in fourteen to fifteen hours a day. The former owners were three brothers; but we were only two. On top of it all, we realized that we had to continue the delivery service, but we did not drive.

We bought an old car. Dave, who was temporarily out of work, came to work with us, did the deliveries and taught Grandpa to drive. When we told Eva we had bought a car, she would not believe it. We took her down and showed her the jalopy (that's what it was). She stared at it with an incredulous expression. Her reaction really expressed the turn our lives had taken: unreachable things had now become possible. Dave would pick us up every morning, drive us to the store, and take us home at night. The day before he had to go back to work, Grandpa passed the driving test. That is how close we cut everything in those days.

It took us most of the first year to master the business and pay off our debts (with the exception of the money we owed Emery). All of our plans did not materialize, however. I had planned to be at the store only part time and we had hoped to rent an apartment in Bay Ridge. Neither of these things was possible at first. A loosely organized cash business like ours was could not afford to have a stranger at the register. Since Grandpa was either working the machines in the back or was out, I had to spend long hours at the store. To get an affordable apartment in the highly desirable Bay Ridge proved impossible, so we continued to live close to an hour's ride away from the store. (By subway, it took two hours to get there!) Either way, I had to be away all day. But there was no turning back. Our future and Emery's money were riding on this venture.

We engaged housekeepers, one after the other, but they were less than satisfactory. Neighbors pitched in. But they were only a stop-gap measure.

Everyone we knew was looking for an apartment for us, but without success. Then summer came and with it a temporary solution. A friend of ours ran a summer camp for children in Montreal. Five children from our extended family were going. Their ages ranged from two years older than Eva to seven weeks younger than Jackie. We thought it was a good idea to send our two also. Grandpa and Emery drove them up to camp. I welcomed the opportunity to stay in bed and rest.

Then a ray of hope appeared in our search for an apartment. Across the street from our store, Charlie Abdo ran a factory. He made bathrobes. Above the store, he had remodeled a railroad apartment for his family, but that spring, he purchased a new house in Montauk, Long Island. He promised us that if, at the end of the summer, his family liked it there, we could have the apartment. In the middle of August, he said we could have the apartment the first of September!

But at the end of August, he changed it to the first of October. His wife needed another month to make up her mind. What a dilemma! What to do? The fall season was upon us, the hardest three months in the business, which financially make or break the year. We were still up to our eyebrows in debt. I had to be there from early morning till late at night. This meant we had to leave Grove Street before the children awoke and get home after they had gone to bed. If there was an emergency, it would take me two hours to get home, since I did not drive. We knew the help we could get was not the best. We had to make the hardest decision of our lives: to leave the children in Canada to stay with our friends there. These people took care of children in their home and we knew that our children would be well cared-for, well fed, and safe.

How did I feel when I saw the other children come home from school? I could not afford to acknowledge or give vent to my emotions, so I suppressed them. I walked around with a lump in the pit of my stomach and constantly suffered from migraines. Today we hear of people who are traumatized by a disaster, an act of God or man, receiving immediate therapy or other psychological help. No one—including us—thought of that. Nor could we have afforded such a luxury had we thought of it!

October 1 came and Charlie's wife was still not ready to give up the apartment. On October 11, Grandpa's birthday, the children called from Canada. Eva, who understood the situation and, until then, had been very upbeat, said, with tears in her voice, "Mom, we want to come home; please bring us home."

It was a Monday. I remember going to the bank to make a deposit and crying all the way. I was still crying when I stopped at Charlie's store and completely lost control. "It just is not fair that you should have two homes and I can't have my children," I screamed. I went on and on. He was a kind, good-natured man. He just stared at me and then said, "I don't care what my wife says; my children like it on Long Island, so the apartment is yours."

We moved in the next day and, the following day, we flew the children home. (To go for them ourselves would have meant to wait for Sunday. And besides, we could not have made the round-trip drive in one day.) We drove to La Guardia Airport to meet them. On the way, our jalopy overheated. Then we overshot the exit and ended up in Kew Gardens. Frantic, we called Joe. He went to the airport, but it took him awhile to get there and so my poor kids landed in the airport alone; we were not there to greet them. Jackie was so nervous, he stuttered for a day. We couldn't even make out what he was saying. But our children were home! The next morning at 8 o'clock, Charlie Abdo pulled the master switch at his factory below our apartment and eighty sewing machines started their noisy racket, continuing until five o'clock at night. Six days a week, rain or shine.

It was noisy. Most of the rooms were windowless. But it was home for seven years. We were together—working just across the street. The children stopped in at the store on the way to and from school or play. We knew that if we worked hard (and we did), better things would be ahead for us.

Our aims were modest and we achieved them. First and foremost, we wanted to give our children a good education, so that they could have an easier and better life than we had. We wanted to buy a house, to give them a comfortable home to dream their dreams in. We wanted to travel, to see the world, this time in comfort—not because we had to but because we wanted to.

We strove to make conservative investments, to achieve financial independence. We wanted to be able to pursue any interest we may have and live anywhere we wished in our old age.

Sweet Jordan and Lauren, life is not always fair or just or kind. You cannot judge anything or anyone by your standards alone. Life cannot be measured by the luxuries one has. Nor can parental love be measured by the luxuries a parent gives a child. Being willing to sacrifice for one's children and for the family is not a guarantee for success. When you are as preoccupied with survival as I have been since my teens, you must take your chances and hope for the best. Have I always done the right thing? I doubt it.

If only I had been a better child. If only I had gone with my family to the ghetto, I could have been a help to them. And I may have survived anyway. If only I had not become pregnant right away, I would not have been so preoccupied with my own welfare, I could have helped my fellow sufferers when they returned from the concentration camps. If only we had not been so impatient and waited a little longer until our children were a little older to "make it in America." If only, if only. . . ." But these are choices only hindsight can afford.

Life is like a game of cards. You are dealt a hand and you have two options: you either play out the hand or throw in the cards. I never considered the latter. I found that life at its worst was precious and worth living. A beautiful sunset, a colorful flower garden or a kitten basking in the sunshine is exciting and wonderful, even if viewed from an attic window. And there is always hope for a brighter tomorrow.

So I played the hand I was dealt to the best of my ability. I never looked back. When we left a town or a country, that was that. If the place we came to was less hospitable, less luxurious than the one we left behind, so be it. Yesterday was history. What mattered was today and what we did with it, and that we were finally all safe and secure behind that light in the window.

Epilogue

About twenty years ago, I had a conversation with a friend of a good friend of mine. During the conversation, he asked me about my experiences in Auschwitz. When I told him that I wasn't there, that I was in hiding during the war, he was amazed and asked, "Don't your friends know anything about you?"

I realized that the answer was "No." My friends in Bay Ridge, where we had lived for years (and were active members at the Jewish Center), knew nothing of our wartime experiences, nor about the family I lost. It struck me that I had locked the pain of that loss in my heart, and their pictures in the briefcase that my mother sent after me so many years ago. And so I did two things: First, I took a family picture and some other pictures of individual family members, framed them, and hung them on the wall alongside the staircase leading to the upper floor of my house. Second, I sat down and wrote the story of my family members, describing their fate and mine during the war. I presented my story at a Sisterhood meeting.

I continue to talk about my family and my wartime experiences every chance I get. And now I am sharing the story of our family with you, my grandchildren.

I have learned something from telling my story. I have learned that I had been hiding my family not only from others but from myself as well. I had not been able to bare to face the loss. When I attend a funeral where a friend or relative had lost a loved one, while I express my sympathies, I wonder if they know how lucky they are to be able to mourn their loved ones, to have had the privilege to care for them and, now that they had died, to bury them, to weep over them, and have a gravesite to visit.

Of all the unbearable horrors that have befallen my family, the fact that nothing remains of them, that I had no time to mourn, nowhere to direct my grief, has been, for me, the hardest thing to bear. One day, I was surrounded by a loving family; the next day I was ushered out of my door, never to see them again. Where are they? I can never say, "My mother, may she rest in peace," and know where she is.

Where are they? They are locked in my heart, like a heavy stone pressing in the pit of my stomach—and in my dreams and nightmares.

Putting their pictures on my walls and writing about them in this book for you, Jordan and Lauren, has been my way to place that hurt into the open and learn to deal with it. And, of course, this book has given me the opportunity to share my earlier life with you.